TEA

OF A

TOWN

Written by

Shelley Hinchliffe-Reece

Cover design by

Jayden Hinchliffe

With thanks to Karen for the support on all three books and for keeping me on track when I've doubted myself along the way

For my Oscar & Jayden

Never give up on your dreams

Chapter 1

19th May 2019

A wicker casket lays silently in front of the red velvet curtains with an old and grubby but much loved fish tail parka draped across the top. A few slightly wilting red roses sit on the end as the priest says a few kind words to finish the service.

"And as we say goodbye, we remember a life that was mostly colourful and sometimes solitary but always interesting." His voice echoes loudly.

Shell and her dear old friend Giff sit firmly perched on the end of the front bench. Both feeling the need to be as close to each other as possible.

"You ok babe?" He asks, quietly taking her hand.

"Yeah I'm alright, it's all a bit final though." She replies with a soft voice and her hands shaking a little.

Daz and Lou sit alongside them with Sam and Tomo on the end. The crematorium echoes slightly and is empty except for the six of them paying their respects to an old friend.

The line of black Harringtons is looking smart and meaningful on them all with every one of them staring down towards their shiny Doc Martens and deep in thought of the loss they've had to deal with. It makes them all think hard about their own mortality and gives them a need to live the rest of their lives to the full.

'You're Wondering Now' by The Specials comes on at Shell's request and the little curtains start to open. The casket slides along slowly and peacefully out of sight and Shell feels a stray tear run down her cheek. Wiping it away with her sleeve, she sings along to the last of the song lyrics gently with her mates and smiles at the memories running through her mind.

"Come here you." Says Giff, taking her in his arms. "Death is really shit but it happens to us all so the best we can do is be there for each other at the end."

"Yeah it's a bit fuckin' sad when you end up with just six at your funeral though, hey?" Replies Shell, parking her head on his shoulder. "It's not about how many attend ya know. It's about the quality of friendship with the ones that are still there Shell." Says Giff, feeling an inner strength taking over.

"Come on you lot." He says, parting slightly from her to round up the others. "Let's go and have a beer down the road at that little pub we passed on the way in.

*****

The six of them thank the priest politely as they look across to the closed curtains for the last time and head off for a stroll to clear their heads and drown their sorrows together. "That was tough going, sitting through that!" Says Lou, linking arms tightly with Daz. "I didn't think I'd get so bloody emotional."

"It's just death in general." Replies Tomo. "It makes us stop and think how long we've got left ourselves. We're getting on a bit now down the fifties route. Shit, that's fuckin' old. Look at us lot all hanging on to our little bit of youth we have left. Daz isn't in the best of health these days either. We just have to grab life by the bollocks, right until the end!"

Sam kisses him gently on the cheek.

"Love you man!"

Tomo smiles a little at his girl's kiss. Still in love with her after so many years.

Reaching the pub, the group wander in and head straight for the bar. 'Lively Up Yourself' by Bob Marley is playing and the girls all smile together at the top tune.

"Six pints then you lot?" Asks Giff.

They all nod in acceptance and head off to get a table big enough to take them all and Giff carefully walks over with a tray full of beers for everyone to take their share.

"Cheers mate!" Says Daz, holding up his glass.

"Yeah cheers Giff!" The others all join in together.

"Here's to old Carnage!" Says Daz, standing up and clinking his glass with everyone. "He gave us a lot of nightmares over the years but was definitely one of us and didn't deserve to die out there in the cold on his own."

"To Carnage!" They all shout, lifting their glasses once again and clanking them together.

The group all take a long swig on their pints and breathe deeply.

"Trouble is, he chose to live that way and there was nothing we could do." Says Sam. "You lot tried so hard to help when you found him but he didn't want it."

"Yeah you're right." Replies Daz, nodding his head. "You can't help someone unless they want to be helped."

"Deffo!" Adds Giff. "All those memories we have though, hey? Can't imagine life without Carnage back then. I mean, he's given us the funniest and craziest ones to keep forever. Do you lot remember the night we all went out to Wagtails Holiday Camp along the seafront and he tagged along causing his usual nightmares for us? Oh and that poor geezer on the gate hey!"

"Oh man, yeah I remember." Laughs Shell. "Pete was doing the Tiki Disco there and Carnage got us in through security. We started off drinking a bottle of cider as usual in the beach shelter. Oh the memories! They will be stuck in my mind and my heart forever!"

*****

1981

Best mates Giff and Tomo slouch on the damp wooden bench at the grubby beach shelter on the cliffs, sharing a large bottle of Woodpecker cider as they wait for the rest of the gang to arrive. The stench of nights gone by makes them grimace a little.

"Some fucker's spewed up in here it fuckin' stinks!" Says Giff, gagging a little.

"Yeah probably the girls been nickin' cherry B and babysham from home again the lightweights!" Replies Tomo, giggling to himself.

Giff laughs loudly. "Could do with a snog right now. Get me tongue down one of the girl's throats hey."

"New Sta-Press mate?" Asks Tomo, passing the bottle and burping loudly.

"Oh yeah! Fuckin' smart as hell Tom. Lookin' hot tonight my friend, all ready to take my choice of fanny. They'll be gaggin' for me!"

Giff has a long swig on the bottle and takes out a little penknife to start carving his name on the tatty wooden bench as he always does.

'GIFF WOZ ERE eating fanny 81'

"Gotta leave my name for all to see everywhere I go!" He says, smirking with confidence. "That'll do nicely. This is turning into my own bench wiv all my carvings now!"

Daz pulls up sharply on his bike with a huge smirk across his face. Opening the zip of his Harrington jacket, he pulls out a handful of cigarette packets.

"Here ya go lads, twenty Lambert & Butler each. Well, seventeen actually, not the full packs. I did the machine at the pub last night. Easy man! We're all smoked up for the night."

"Top man Daz!" Says Giff, unwrapping the cellophane with a smile.

"You're the top dog!" Adds Tomo, giving Daz a man hug.

"All part of the service." Replies Daz, looking extremely pleased with himself. "Where are the girls then?"

"They'll be here soon enough. Probably choosin' their best frilly knickers ready for a night on the town with *me* of course!" Chuckles Giff, looking pretty certain. "Someone will be suckin' hard tonight!"

The lads all laugh loudly together as Daz grabs the bottle and downs a large mouthful of cider with it dripping down his chin.

*****

Shell, Lou and Sam wander on down towards the beach in anticipation of their night out with the lads. Dressed in their favourite Fred Perry tops and jeans, they all walk tall feeling cool and smart as they go.

"Wanna smoke you two?" Asks Shell, pulling out ten number 6 and a box of swan matches.

"Yeah go on then. I'm skint at the moment you two so gonna have to nick yours tonight." Says Lou, looking a bit fed up.

"That's cool mate I'm sorted and so is Sam aren't you girl?" Says Shell, tapping her mate on the shoulder with the matches.

"Yeah no worries Lou. I've got my money from my Tote round and loads of tips today. Plenty of smokes and here have a mojo I've got pockets full." Laughs Sam, throwing sweets at her mates.

"Nice one you two. Here, I've nicked some Vodka from me dad's cabinet and put a bit of orange squash in it. Have a swig and get us in the mood." Giggles Lou, pulling out a pale blue tuppaware beaker from her bag and peeling off the plastic lid gently.

The girls all laugh loudly at the sight of the sealable cup but take turns in swigging from it and finish it pretty sharpish between them as they arrive at the shelter on the cliff.

"Hey sexy gorgeous females get your arses down here and show us your top tits while I get in your knickers and check out what's on offer tonight!"

"Fuck all on offer for you boy, keep ya hands out!" Shouts Shell, giggling madly and whacking him on the arm.

"Ah come on girls I'm gaggin' for it now. Gonna get your knickers off at Waggies if we get in there for sure!"

"Come on then let's get down there and find a way in." Says Sam, looking ready for anything.

"Yeah ready to go you lot?" Adds Daz, tucking the rest of his smokes in his Harrington.

"Ready, let's do this!" Shouts Tomo, walking out in front with a spring in his step.

*****

"Oh shit, here comes Carnage!" Says Shell, checking him out ahead.

"Alright mate?" Says Giff, patting him on the back with a cheeky laugh.

"Yeah, you off to Waggies you lot? I'm comin', I'll get you in no problem." Replies Carnage, looking full of mischief as always.

"Nice one. How ya gonna do that then mate?" Asks Daz.

"Just watch me!" He replies with a smirk and a swagger.

Reaching the entrance with anticipation, Carnage bolts under the barrier and grabs hold of the little skinny security fella in his little guard box. Grappling with him, he manages to pull out an old kids skipping rope from his pocket and wraps it around the stunned looking chap's arms and body, tying him to his chair.

The rest of the gang laugh loudly at the sight and run as fast as their feet will carry them under the flimsy wooden barrier and up the main path towards the Tiki disco.

Carnage sticks a lump of gaffer tape on to the petrified fella's mouth and runs off in fits of laughter as the old guy sweats profusely in both anger and fright.

The gang head into the disco and spot Pete up above in the music cave. He gives them a wink and a wave and gets ready to stick on some sounds for his mates.

The disco is dark and sweaty and buzzing with eager holiday makers.

Heading for the bar, Daz gets a beer for each of them knowing he looks the oldest by far and easily gets served.

"What the fuck happened to Carnage then? Where's he gone for fuck's sake?" Asks Shell, as the girls all hang out in the corner of the disco, making it their own space.

"He fucked up the security bloke then disappeared!" Replies Sam, giggling with her mates and her beer dribbling down her Fred Perry T-shirt as she snorts with laughter.

The boys wander over with the rest of the beers for everyone, feeling cool and ready for action.

"Make em' last you lot. We ain't got much cash left tonight." Says Giff, handing them round.

Pete wanders over from the side door of the DJ's hole in the wall.

"Alright you lot?" He asks, with a wink.

"Yeah, what ya up to mate?" Replies Giff, lifting his beer towards his pal to acknowledge him.

"The other DJ, Jamie Bull is up there. He's fuckin' about and fingering one of the campers on the chair. I'm keepin' out the way for a bit!" He laughs, screwing his face up slightly.

The lads all laugh and start to wolf-whistle up to the hole in the wall, distracting Jamie as he raises his middle finger down to the crowd with a dirty smirk on his face.

As the end of 'Enola Gay' by OMD fades, 'Lip Up Fatty' by Bad Manners begins to blast out of the huge speakers and Giff and Tomo pull down their braces to below their waist and grab Daz for big skanking time on the dancefloor.

The girls put down their beers quickly and follow, leaping in the air and loving being with the lads out on the floor.

Dripping with sweat and full of adrenaline, the boys wipe their foreheads on their sleeves and keep moving as 'Too Much Too Young' by The Specials follows on and all six of them sing at the top of their voices and take over the full dancefloor for the duration of the track.

As the tune ends, Shell glances out of the window and spots Carnage hurling a rock at the small glass panel of one of the pale blue chalet doors opposite.

Rounding up her mates, they sprint outside just as he is making a run for it with a cassette recorder from inside and two hefty security guys trying their best to keep up but with little success due to their large guts hanging over their jeans and shortness of breath from their smoke filled lungs. Carnage flies like a whippet out of sight within a few seconds.

"Fuckin' hell, that boy will be in deep shit if he's caught but look at him go! They haven't got a hope in hell of catching up." Says Shell, laughing loudly with her mates.

"What a man!" Shout's Giff. "He's got a top Panasonic cassette player there too by the look of it."

They all laugh loudly as they watch him disappear out of sight into the many rows of holiday chalets with his arms full.

*****

The gang head back into the bar area of the disco and hang around in the corner with their beers as 'Karma Chameleon' by Culture club blasts out and all the young girls on their holidays dance around their handbags on the floor.

The disco is heaving now. Hot and sweaty bodies leap around. The room is made to look like a straw shack with lines of hula necklaces and plastic palm trees along the wall with barmaids floating around with flowers in their hair.

"Where's Lou gone?" Asks Shell, Her blue eyes scouring the room intensely.

"Shall we go and check the loos?" Replies Sam, already walking off.

The two girls enter the ladies toilets and immediately hear faint sounds of giggling and grunting noises from the end cubicle.

The door is left ajar so Sam pushes it open a little and pokes her head round to see the edge of Lou sitting on the toilet and Lee 'Lanky' Johnson from school standing with his groin facing her head, pounding backwards and forwards on the open crutch of his jeans.

Catching sight of Sam, Lanky whacks his head on the old flushing chain hanging from the cistern above. Being one of the tallest at school he looks quite awkward in the cubicle.

"Ahhh FUCK!" He shouts, twisting around in the tiny room. "Get the fuck out you dickheads!"

Lou looks rather red in the face and Sam is unsure if it's from the heat or from the speed of her task with Lanky.

"Sorry you two. Enjoy yourselves." Shouts Sam, giggling as she quickly closes the door and runs off with Shell telling her what she's seen.

"What's it taste like Lou girl?" Shouts Shell, popping her head back round the main door and falling about laughing again with her mate.

The girls head back to the Tiki to find the other lads and to fill them in with what they have seen.

*****

In the disco the girls make their way through the crowd while 'Antmusic' by Adam and the Ants blasts out with young girls strutting around the dance floor, imitating all the dance moves they have seen on Top of the Pops on a Thursday evening.

As the girls push their way through the crowd, they spot someone virtually naked spread out in the middle of the dancefloor. As they get closer they notice he has just his pants and socks on and some young girls are pouring beer into his mouth from up high, spilling it everywhere.

Shell looks closer and sees that it's Carnage looking totally spaced out after taking a pink panther acid tab and completely losing the plot.

Lou pops up from behind looking a little sheepish after her bit of fun in the loos.

"Oh my god what the hell is he up to now?" She asks, getting hold of his leg and pulling him to one side of the dancefloor.

"Get the fuck off him you lot!"

"Dunno where he's put the stuff he nicked from the chalets either." Says Shell, helping Lou to stand him up.

As they finally get him to his feet he starts to gag and throws up right across the floor hitting the little crowd of young holiday makers and covering their handbags with projectile vomit and stinking of old fermented cider as it lands.

Some of the girls start to cry while others find it hilarious and run off laughing at him.

Shell and her friends all gather quickly and together they all get him to his feet. They drag him from the dancefloor across to the door as the bar manager storms over shouting about the state of his inflatable palm trees dripping with the stench of yellow vomit. He is closely followed by two pretty young hula girls with the same vomit all spurted up their tan coloured tights and splatters clinging to their little black pumps.

"Get this digusting individual out of here and you are all barred from the camp. I know who you are and you are most definitely not holiday makers! Out Now before I call the police!" He slams, shaking with rage.

The gang swiftly move out with Carnage dragged behind them. They drop him out on the path and begin to chuckle as they all run towards a hole in the fence, briefly glancing behind to check if Carnage still looks alive.

"Not stayin' to take no shit for Carnage, he's a dick!" Shouts Daz, still giggling madly.

"Yeah, fuckin idiot he'll find his way home." Laughs Shell, grabbing Sam's arm and clambering out of the hole in the wire fence.

"Now to find that Panasonic cassette player he nicked!" Shouts Giff, looking shifty. "Finders keepers hey you lot!"

*****

"Oh man, what memories we have hey!" Says Giff, supping the last of his pint and looking around the table at his ageing friends and feeling quite emotional.

"Well, that's one of us gone. Dunno who will be next but we have to look out for each other now, hey." Replies Shell, holding Giff's hand for a moment.

"When can we meet again then you lot?" Asks Tomo, tapping his empty pint glass.

"How about we check out what bands are playing and get a top night out sorted?" Says Lou, excitedly.

"I'll get on to it soon as I get home." Replies Shell, getting up from her chair and pushing away her empty glass.

The gang all agree and hug each other tightly before heading for the door and going their separate ways.

"Love you all forever!" Shouts Shell, turning back with a little tear in her eye.

"Love you more!" Shouts Lou, smiling broadly.

"Snog you all soon!" Declares Giff, with a very cheeky grin.

"Later you lot!" Shouts Tomo and Sam in unison.

"Can't wait for next time you crazy lot!" Daz shouts lovingly.

"How about we meet at the CO-OP for some chocolate!"

"See ya next week when I hit London!" Bellows Giff, blowing a kiss to Shell.

They all laugh loudly in the distance loving the bond that continues to live on all these years later.

Chapter 2

"This is weird hey mate?" Says Shell, linking arms with Giff as they jump off the tube in West London.

"Suppose it is a bit." He replies, smiling. "I finally get to see where you live after about forty years! So what happened with Marty then? Why didn't he come to the funeral?"

"Well, since we had that beach reunion a few years back, I'd been seeing him at weekends for a while. We couldn't live together though. As you know, I hated it down there and he hated it up here but we had something quite special so we kept it going. My life changed so much over the last few years. It all stopped after a while. He gave me an ultimatum basically. Move in with him down there or we pack it in!" Shell sighs. "I can't live there, I despise it. This is my home. Anyway, he doesn't speak to me now. Weird how it goes, hey?"

"I don't see him either mate. He must be hiding away!" Replies Giff, looking slightly puzzled by his disappearance. "Blimey, your life has been pretty colourful girl? And what's Dan up to now then?"

"He moved out of our little home a few years back. I don't think he's seeing anyone else after all that shit with Jess Middleton. He's quite a stable fella our Dan. Well, where relationships are concerned, he certainly is. He has a little flat not far from me. I miss him badly and all his music and banter. I fucked that up real bad didn't I?"

Giff gives her a slight smile and an arm around her back.

"Can't change the past babe. Only make a better future." He says, kindly.

They arrive at the house and Shell puts the key in the door.

"Come in mate." She says, untying her laces in the doorway and slinging her shiny, cherry boots to one side. "I'll get some beers out and we can listen to some sounds if you fancy."

"Yeah nice." He replies, taking off his own Docs and Harrington.

Shell wanders off to the kitchen and grabs a couple of bottles from the fridge.

"Here ya go. What shall we listen to then?" She says, heading for the lounge.

"How about some of our top Ska tunes or some rockin' reggae?" Replies Giff, looking a little loved up at the thought of great sounds on the sofa with her.

"I'll stick on some Selecter. Some of the best! I remember dancing in the beach shelter with you to this just before I left."

She puts the ipod on shuffle and 'Missing Words' comes on. Giff starts rocking to the music on the sofa, feeling content with his old friend by his side.

"Fuckin' hell, I feel like I'm sixteen again sittin' here wiv you girl. God how did we get here to this age!" He says, quietly shaking his head.

"Come on, dance with me." Says Shell, dragging him up by the arm. "Age is fuck all. We are still the same best mates, just a bit slower."

Putting their beers down on the table, they do a little gentle skanking to the great sounds and smile at one another throughout the song with no words needed.

As the next track starts up, Shell wraps her arms around his neck while moving to the music. 'Special Brew' by Bad Manners pours out of the system to their delight.

Giff responds by grabbing her round the waist and staring straight into her eyes. He takes his smiling mouth and plants a heavy kiss on her lips.

"Oh shit!" He says, checking for a reaction. "I don't think I should've done that but I really wanted to. I've always wondered about us, whether we should've been more than mates. I tried *well* hard to get in your pants!"

She takes his face in her hands and gently kisses him back with a smile, continuing to dance to the music.

"We stay best mates Giff. Never change that, sweet man. Anything more will change us forever."

"Dammit!" He laughs, cheekily. "I'll go to my grave wondering girl!"

'My Girl' by Madness comes on and the two of them flop down on the sofa hugging and laughing together happily, as they always did as kids.

"Cheers babe. Love ya more than anything in this world." She says, wrapping her arm around his shoulder and clinking their bottles together. "Nothing can ever take our friendship away. It's lifelong. We go back a million years!"

"Still fancy the arse off ya though." He giggles, trying to get his hand in her T-shirt. "Come on, you know you want me really."

"You're such a fucker." She laughs. "I'll give you a scrap. You're sex mad aren't ya?"

"Yep and I've spent a lifetime trying to get past your belt!"

"hahaha! Hey, remember when we nearly got it on that day, way back when we were fifteen?" Asks Shell, with her reminiscent head on. "Before I even went out with Marty and it was just us lot hangin' out."

"Shit yeah, I nearly got you at Tommy Gates' house party but you chickened out on me. Fuckin' Gatesy's fault. You were mad for him, weren't ya?"

"Yeah, he was the most gorgeous boy I'd ever set eyes on. Oh the memories, from about the age of thirteen I couldn't take my eyes off him and followed him everywhere. All to no avail though, He never even looked at me like that, we were always just top mates and up to no good. I've always thought about him throughout my life. I look at his picture in my old photo album sometimes and wonder what might've been and where he ended up. "

Then you met Marty and the rest is history!" Says Giff, with half a smile. "Oh man, I remember meeting up at the bench along the seafront. Carnage was causing his usual chaos all night and then heading off to Gatesy's gaff for another top night... Oh and MANDY JESSOP!!!...

*****

1980

"Alright you lot?" Says Shell, wandering up to the park bench with her two best friends, Lou and Sam.

"Hey, good to see some top totty for my night to begin!" Replies Giff, grabbing the cheek of her backside. "I'm gonna shag ya stupid tonight, especially in that red Fred Perry. Oh yes!"

"Get real arsehole!" Slams Shell, whacking him on the arm.

"Just watch me, I'm tellin' ya, I'll have ya gaggin' for me by the time we get to the party. What's that stink on you lot anyway?"

"Impulse." Says Lou, looking proud of her overpowering aroma and pulling out the little gold spray can, pointing it in his direction.

"Keep that shit off me." He shouts, pushing her arm down to the floor to get away. "I've got the best Brut 33 on tonight so hold on tight girls, you're in for the ride of your lives!"

The girls all snigger at him and give him a dig on the arm.

"You see? All that impulse, you're all up for it. Just wait til we get there, I'll do you all. Take you from behind and show you a good time." He says, trying to stick his tongue in Shell's ear.

"Oh shut the fuck up Giff." She replies, giggling madly at his constant barrage of sexual advances.

Grabbing her arms, he pushes her across the top of the bench, laughing uncontrollably with Tomo. Bending her over, he begins hammering his groin against her backside as he pretends to whip like riding horseback.

The mates all fall about laughing as Shell clambers up, waving a big stick at him.

"I'll shove this stick up your arse in a minute! Come on dickhead, let's get down to Gatesy's house. His mum and dad are out til after midnight. It's gonna be a right laugh."

"Come on then you lot for fuck's sake!" Says Tomo, looking ready to leave and eagerly grabbing his bottle of Merrydown cider.

Giff picks up his pack of Long Life Lager and they all head off. The gang all still giggling at Giff's antics.

"Can't believe I'm going to Tommy Gates' house." Sighs Shell, with a loved up smile. "Any chance I can get and I'm there."

"You're fuckin' mad on him, Shell. Have you asked him out?" Says Lou, intrigued by Shell's obsession for Gatesy.

"Nah, I'm too scared but he's so gorgeous. Those eyes!"

"Oh god, you're like a puppy all excited." Giggles Sam. "He's always in trouble mate, ya know?"

"Couldn't give a shit. I love a boy with a bit of excitement. None of that boring stuff. He ain't interested in me anyway. Never takes a second look. I could dance on his bed in me knickers and Docs and he'd walk past and have a smoke!" She chuckles, with a hint of sadness.

The girls all laugh loudly at the thought of her parading on his bed.

"Wanna juicy fruit girls?" Asks Sam, pulling out the yellow packet from her pocket and passing them around.

"Hey, we're here too ya know. Give us one ya tight arse."
Says Giff, running to catch up from behind.

He and Tomo grab a chewing gum and the five of them stroll down the seafront towards the turning for Gatesy's house.

"Marty Clark asked me out yesterday." Says Shell, raising her eyebrows. "I can't decide what to do. He's quite a looker too but then there's Gatesy. Shit he's to die for! He wore a ski jumper to school today. Oh man, so much in love!"

"Fuck Shell, snap out of it girl." Replies Lou. "Marty Clark is well handsome. He would treat you well better than Gatesy."

"I know but he's not as good lookin' and he's probably a bit of a safe bet. Tommy Gates is more exciting for sure. You know me, I need a bit of craziness in my life!"

"Oh fuck, she's in love big time." Laughs Lou, shaking her head.

"You don't need any of them Shell, you got all of my body any time you want it." Shouts Giff, gyrating his hips with his hand held high. "I can be as exciting as you want. I'll give you it all tonight and you'll be in heaven."

"Bit of Merrydown cider and he will look like anyone you want!" Laughs Tomo, patting his mate on the shoulder. "He's such a looker after ten pints."

Hysterical laughter rings out through the gang and Giff stands proud taking it all on the chin.

"Where's Daz anyway?" Asks Lou, striding out in front of the others. "He must have something to take with us. He never lets us down."

"He'll be there. He'll turn up in a minute ready for action." Says Tomo. "Who's going to this party then? Do we know them all?"

"Gatesy will have all sorts there. He's in with loads of people round here." Replies Shell. "I bet Mandy Jessop is there trying to get off with every boy she can grab hold of!"

The group all turn to look as they hear Daz shouting from behind on his bike.

"Hey fuckers, what's happenin'?" He bellows loudly.

Circling the road on his bike, he is carrying four fishing nets in various colours across his shoulder and a yellow bucket and spade in the shape of a castle hanging from the handlebar.

"What the fuck are you up to man?" Shouts Giff, chuckling at the sight before him.

He pulls up next to them with a huge grin on his face as always.

"I saw them outside the beach stores just hangin' there so I whipped them on to me bike and thought we could go tadpoling first before the party."

The gang laugh loudly at him and his stupid ideas.

Finding the whole thing too hilarious, Tomo lays on the floor crying and holding his belly.

"Come on, over the boating lake it will be a laugh." Says Daz, holding up the nets and turning his bike round. "I've only got four but that'll do for us lot."

"Alright, let's do it then." Says Sam. "It's early yet and we can have a laugh over there."

Heading off across the road and holding a net each, the fits of laughter continue as Shell presses play on her cassette and 'Food for Thought' By UB40 comes on to keep them dancing along to the edge of the lake.

"I'm the fuckin' top man!" Shouts Daz, holding up his bucket and spade and giggling loudly.

"Can't believe I'm off fishing when I'm meant to be at a fuckin' party." Laughs Lou.

The girls all chuckle together linking arms and swaying the fishing nets around in the air.

As they arrive, Daz throws down his bike and half fills the bucket with water, scooping it up in the dank green liquid on the lake.

"Love doin' this." Says Daz, dipping one of the nets in and finding a couple of silver fish to throw into the bucket.

Shell presses play again on the cassette recorder and 'Night Boat to Cairo' By Madness pumps out.

Discarding the nets quickly, the six of them leap up and start to skank around the bucket, singing at the top of their voices.

"Ah top tune Shell." Says Giff, downing a glug of cider and swirling one of the nets around again in the lake.

"Here we go!" He says, happily pulling out a couple of tadpoles for the bucket.

"Alright tossers?"Comes a voice from behind.

Carnage has arrived and has sneaked up behind them to check out their stash of alcohol and to see what's in the bucket.

"What's happenin' man?" Asks Daz, sipping on a can of Skol Lager.

"Headin' to Gatesy's. You lot comin?"

"Yeah after this." Laughs Tomo, filling the bucket with more tadpoles.

'Hands Off, She's Mine' By The Beat blasts out of the little player and the nets are discarded once again while the gang all leap around to their favourite music. Singing at the top of their voices, they are oblivious to Carnage leaving them to it and legging it up the road.

"Ah man, I fuckin' love that song." Says Daz, picking up his net again for a dip in the lake. "What the fuck's this in me bucket then?"

"Oh what!" Shouts Giff. "That fuckhead Carnage, he's topped up the bucket with the rest of the Merrydown."

"Pissed up tadpoles." Giggles Tomo. "Out of their fuckin' heads!"

The rest of them start to laugh and see the funny side of it.

"Come on you lot let's head off to the party hey?" Says Daz, emptying the bucket in the lake.

"Nooooo!" Shouts Giff. "Your gettin' the rest of the lake pissed now ya fuckin' knobhead."

The girls are all on floor by now rolling around and crying with laughter.

"Oh my god, stop will ya." Splutters Sam. "My stomach is hurting."

Giff gives Daz a dig in the back and all of them start to sword fight with the fishing nets, havin' a good laugh at their antics before heading off up the road towards Gatesy's place for the evening.

*****

The back door is ajar as they arrive and step inside the bungalow. The kitchen is already bursting with young teens in tiny groups dotted around.

Mandy Jessop is already doing her best to get off with Gatesy. Sitting on the kitchen worktop with her ample bust popping out of a tightly fitting boob tube and giving him the come on at every opportunity.

"Alright Gatesy?" Asks Shell, throwing him off the scent of Mandy for a moment.

"Yeah, wanna line wiv me Shell?"

"Oh yeah course I do!" She replies, eagerly following him to his bedroom and sending one of her dirty looks in the direction of the Jessop girl.

Sitting on his single bed, she takes in the smell of him on his pillow and smiles a little as she watches him chopping white powder on The Specials album cover.

Longing for him to want to sit with her, she waits patiently.

"Here ya go girl, have a sniff of that. Good stuff will knock ya backwards."

Shell gets up and takes the rolled up pound note and snorts the line quickly from Terry Hall's head on the album sleeve.

"Oh man!" She says, taking it deeply into her nose and throat and getting a cold rush to her head. "Nice one Gatesy!"

"Come on, let's get amongst the party." He says, quickly hiding his little stash and heading for the bedroom door.

"Ok yeah." She replies, feeling the usual devastation of never getting anywhere near him for a snogging session and wondering why he shows no sign of wanting her for more than friendship.

Looking a little dejected but buzzing and sniffing madly already, she follows him out to the lounge where the music is blasting with 'Hanging on the Telephone' by Blondie and Mandy Jessop has her boob tube off and is shaking her breasts in the face of any boy she can find, including Gatesy as he enters the room.

As usual, Gatesy laughs at her advances and tries to move on but Shell is boiling over and with the whizz hitting her full on now, she swipes a punch up to Mandy's chin and watches as her teeth clatter together and her head rolls backwards, making her lose balance and fall on to the sofa, her large breasts making a slapping noise as they hit her chest bone. Realizing what she has done, Shell jumps backwards and Mandy leaps up from the sofa waving her clenched fist around in the air and sharing an evil look.

Grabbing a handful of Shell's hair, she tugs at it with all her might, trying to swing her round but Shell is having none of it and with the drugs hurling confidence at her, she swipes back again making it a full on scrap.

Tommy Gates laughs a little and wanders off, lighting up a smoke and drifting into the kitchen for a beer.

Giff and Tomo run into the lounge and begin to cheer as Shell knocks her back down to the floor for the second time and raises her fist into the air in triumph.

"What a shot!!" Shouts Giff, grabbing her hand and punching it into the air for a second time.

The three of them leave Mandy to get up and dress herself and watch her squirm as she sees her failure to win. Heading into the middle of the room, the three friends start to skank wildly as Lou puts on a cassette she found up the corner and 'On My Radio' by The Selecter blasts out.

Daz rushes in with Sam on hearing the tune blaring and joins the others taking over the centre of the lounge with their braces hanging loosely below the waist and gleaming Doc Martens leaping around the floor. Laughing and singing at the top of their voices, the mates are unaware that this will be a memory they will carry throughout their lives.

*****

"Good night goin' on here hey Lou?" Says Shell, wandering off to the back door with her mate for some fresh air.

"Yeah apart from fuckin' Jessop. Nice one for landing her one!" Replies Lou chuckling a little.

The girls head off outside and light up a smoke over by the shed.

Hearing clanking noises behind the shed door, Shell peers in through the little window on the side and sees Carnage filling a black school bag with Gatesy's dad's tools.

"Oh for fuck's sake, not stealin' from your mates Carnage. Get the fuck out of there!" She blasts at him through the window.

Briefly looking up, he ties up his bag and pushes the door open quickly.

Lou grabs his arm and tries to bring him down but he's too strong and slippery and makes his getaway with the bulging bag across his shoulder.

"Oh shit! Tommy will go fuckin' mad."

At the front of the house, Gatesy and Giff are doing a spliff on the doorstep as Carnage barges past.

That fucker's got something of mine, I know it. Get him Giff."

The two of them take off at speed after him, shouting all the way.

Carnage kicks over a rubbish bin in front of them like something from Starsky and Hutch and the metal tub clanks down the road, spreading newspapers and vegetable peelings across the street.

Dodging each pile, the lads laugh loudly as Carnage tumbles over an old set of roller skates discarded on the roadside and an angry ginger cat hissing at him as he falls flat on his face and the heavy tools spread across the path with some force behind them.

As Giff and Gatesy arrive at the scene, still laughing at their Starsky and Hutch moment, an old fella picks up Carnage by his ear and marches him off with one arm up his back.

"Fuck! That's Johnny Potter, his uncle. He's a copper." Says Gatesy, breathing heavily and starting to collect up his dad's tools.

"He's in the shit now." Laughs Giff, bending over with a stitch in his belly.

"He's a right fucker ain't he?" Replies Gatesy, still chuckling and hauling the bag on to his back. "Come on man, let's get this shit home. I've got weed to smoke, white powder to sniff and cider to sling down my neck!"

"Let's do it mate." Replies Giff, speeding off before him and making a sniffing gesture back at him with a wink.

*****

Shell, Lou and Sam are skankin' madly in the front room to 'Do Rocksteady' by The Bodysnatchers as Gatesy and Giff arrive back.

The girls are linking arms and singing loudly as their Monkey Boots and Doc Martens leap up and down on the heavily patterned carpet. Both girls are completely in their element with the music playing and glugging on little Cherry B bottles and huge plastic bottles of cheap cider.

Tomo and Daz run in and join them, twanging their braces and leaping around looking smart as hell in their favourite Ben Sherman shirts and Sta-press trousers.

Giff and Gatesy peer into the room with a grin and then head off towards the bedroom to skin up. As they pass Gatesy's mum and dad's room, they hear grunting and giggling and open the door quickly to check out what's going on.

"What the fuck?" Shouts Gatesy.

Giff splutters with laughter as they see Mandy Jessop completely naked, except for her socks, sprawled out on the double bed with rocker Chris Shipman who is licking strawberry Angel Delight from many parts of her ample body and grunting as he does so.

"Get the fuck out of me mum's bed dickheads and keep ya fuckin' hands off the stuff in the fridge. Wankers, get out of it!" Says Gatesy, looking disgusted at the sight in front of him and pulling at the covers to get them off.

Mandy jumps up squealing and looking very pink and creamy as she hurls herself and her wobbling body out of the door to the bathroom.

"Ah you fuckin' spoilers. That was so good man!" Says Chris, pulling up his greying pants and shaking his long greasy hair away from his eyes as he tries to wipe the pink mess off the bed sheets.

"For fuck's sake!" Says Gatesy. "Get your shitty fat arse off me mum's bed and fuck off out my house.

"I'm off. I've had me oats and me dinner." Says a very slurry Chris as he laughs and looks chuffed at his achievements.

Gatesy heads off to his own room with Giff and chops up a line of whizz with a little kitchen knife while Giff rolls a joint.

"Oh man, that was a disgusting sight. She's a fuckin' horror and he's a greasy fuckin' mess." Says Gatesy, screwing up his face as he snorts quickly through the rolled up pound note. "Yeah but he's got the right idea. That Angel Delight looks pretty tasty." Replies Giff, as they both fall into a heap of laughter on the bed.

"That was mine from me tea. I was gonna have it later or tomorrow." Says Gatesy, almost crying with laughter now.

Shell pops her head around the bedroom door wanting to know where the boys are.

"Come and have a sniff Shell if ya want one." Says Gatesy, toking on a joint and trying to calm his laughter.

"I'm in!" Replies Shell, eagerly slamming the door so that no one else comes in and heading straight for the lines of white powder on the side. "Nice one!"

Snorting it fiercely through the now shabby looking, rolled up note, she holds back her head and feels the cold rush through her body.

"Woah, that's good stuff Gatesy." She says, sniffing repeatedly.

"I'm just goin' to get beers from the fridge." Smiles Gatesy, as he heads out the door.

Shell leaps on to the bed next to Giff and gives him a quick hug.

"Oh man, I'm so in love, Giff!"

"What, with *me*?" He replies, smiling and grabbing her round the waist and trying his luck in her jeans.

"No, you div. You know I'm fuckin' mad for Gatesy. He's so gorgeous. I wish he was all mine. I've waited for him for two years and still getting' nowhere."

"Well, if he don't want ya, you can have me any time." He says, trying to wedge his tongue into her mouth as she struggles free.

"Fuck off Giff, you're my mate! You know I've only got to look into Gatesy's eyes and I'm a fucked up mess."

"Ah you're wastin' your time with him. He's more interested in gettin' shitfaced. Come and see me anytime and sit on my face."

The two of them laugh loudly together and start play fighting on the bed as Gatesy comes back in.

"What the fuck you two doin' hey?" He says, giggling at them.

"Shell fancies the arse of ya mate, did ya know?"

Gatesy laughs and throws them both a can of Skol.

"Come on you fuckers." He says, heading for the door again.

"Time to get amongst it and listen to some sounds."

"See?" Says Giff, nudging Shell. "He just wants to get off his face. I'm the one you need for giving you pleasure. Fuck him, give me ya body!"

He grabs her by the backside and tries to stick his tongue in her ear.

"Oh fuck off!" She replies, kneeing him where it hurts and giggling as she follows Gatesy out the door and into the front room.

'Hong Kong Garden' by Siouxsie and the Banshees is blasting out and many of the teens are throwing themselves around the room to the music.

Lou and Sam are huddled in the corner with the music system, waiting patiently to change it to something to skank to and Daz and Tomo are on the other side of the room watching the dancing and swigging from a large bottle of cider between them.

As the track finishes, Lou finds a single of 'Gangsters' by The Specials and eagerly places the vinyl onto the record player.

It blasts out for them and the whole room erupts. Everyone crams into the front room skanking madly. Doc Martens, loafers and Monkey boots shining and leaping crazily, their sweaty drunk bodies loving every moment.

Just as they are all dancing together, one of the party goers enters the room and shouts "Mandy Jessop is on the doorstep naked!"

Shell and Lou roll their eyes and go to the front door to have a look at what's going on. They open the door and see her full body swaying around as her breasts swing from side to side and she rubs them seductively.

"Gatesy fucked me Shell and he said it was the best shag he'd ever had. You're a no go girl. He thinks you're an ugly bitch!" Says Mandy, slurring and then falling around in histerical laughter.

Shell's blood starts to boil and storms across the path landing a punch full on her nose so fierce she didn't know she had it in her.

"Well he won't fuck ya again with a splattered nose will he you fuckin' animal!" Shell roars at the drunken Jessop now flat on the paving slabs of Gatesy's path with her head stuck in his mum's well-trimmed hedge.

Turning to Lou, Shell raises her fist in victory and both of them giggle and run off back to join the party.

"Shell, there's no way that horror slept with Gatesy. He wouldn't touch her with a barge pole!" Laughs Lou, shaking her head and linking arms with her mate.

"I know that. But she needed a slap for sure!" Chuckles Shell. "I dunno where that came from mate. It just rose up inside me and I whacked her!"

"Top shot girl! Right on target!" Shouts Lou, trying to be heard above the music.

As they walk back in to the room, a massive cheer comes from the dancers and the rest of the gang who were all watching from the window.

Shell take a bow and laughs loudly as 'Turning Japanese' by The Vapours is cranked up and the whole room leaps around laughing and singing at the top of their voices.

*****

"Oh my God Giff, what fantastic memories. We could go on for days finding memories like that." Says Shell, hugging her old mate. "We had the best times hey. No one can beat them for sure!"

"Too right girl, we had the top time for growing up. Never change a thing hey!" Giff smiles and hugs her tightly. "It's been the best night sitting here reminiscing with ya. I'm so happy we are all together again even if it has taken too long."

"Gonna sort a good night out for us all real soon." Says Shell, confidently. "We are all getting on a bit now so gotta make the most of it. Agreed?"

"Totally agree! Love ya girl. Top night tonight

"Love ya more you fuck head" Says Shell, lovingly.

Both laugh and play punch each other as they drink into the night remembering their lives so long ago.

Chapter 3

Shell stands at the kitchen sink waiting for the kettle to boil. Looking out of the window at the bright spring morning. She smiles to herself as she remembers her evening with her lovely old friend and pulls out two mugs to make coffee for them both.

Quietly entering the spare bedroom, she places the drinks on the bedside table and gently kisses his cheek while he starts to stir.

"Hello gorgeous." He says with a big smile and a huge yawn. "Thanks for a top night darlin', it was so good to come up and see you here in your home even though I'm not a huge fan of the dirty old city of London. Let's not leave it another hundred years before the next visit hey!"

"Did you sleep well mate?" She asks, opening the curtains wide to let in the sunshine on a beautiful and cloudless day.

"Like a log darlin'. Too many beers as always but well worth the hangover I'd say."

"It's been amazing having you here in London Giff." She replies with a giggle. We have so many fantastic memories. I just love to recall everything I did with you and the others."

Shell lays down on the side of the bed with him and takes a mouthful of the hot morning coffee from her mug.

"Hey, Do you remember those days when the only things that we thought were important to us were managing to get cider from the offy while under age and making sure we had smokes, cash and the best Fred Perrys." Says Shell, reminiscing and feeling love for her old friend. "And the best music of course from The Specials, The Beat, Madness and so many other top bands back then."

"Of course I remember. Not a fuckin' care in the world as long as I got me hand in the girls knickers!" He laughs.

"Ha! You were such a bad boy. Driving all the girls totally nuts every day at school." Giggles Shell, giving him a little nudge on the arm. "How many of them did you actually manage to get into their pants?"

"Well now, that would be telling." He whispers with a cheeky grin. "Let's just say I did alright!"

"Dirty shitbag!" Replies Shell and they both laugh out loud.

"Nice coffee darlin' but where's me full English breaky? Ya know I'm starvin' for some eggs, bacon, mushrooms, fried bread and anything else you can muster up! What ya got for a growing lad, hey?"

Shell laughs and gives him an elbow nudge in his ribs.

"I'll have my drink and then cook you a very special fry up my friend."

Both lay together feeling content with their world in the moment.

"I keep on having all these memories come back to me about so many more of our times together Giff." Says Shell, looking deep in thought. "I don't know where it comes from but it's just there in my head waiting to be recalled."

"Do you remember the time we all went to town on the train and some of the girls got caught shoplifting? We were the lucky ones and fled the scene with our free shopping! All of us girls were completely mad for all those flavoured lip gloss back then. They had cherry, peppermint, orange and cola. Probably more but those are the ones I remember. Cherry was my favourite. I'm sure we swiped quite a few over time. Never left the house for a disco without a set of gorgeous glistening lips!"

"I can taste it on all of the female pouty lips now." Says Giff, with a smile. "Couldn't beat a minty snog!!!"

"Oh man, yeah that trip turned into a nightmare for some of them. Sam wasn't allowed out for ages after that." Laughs Giff. "How do you keep remembering all this stuff?"

Shell shrugs her shoulders and smiles gently. She gives him another kiss on the cheek and starts to recall the day...

*****

1981

Half awake, Shell looks across her bedroom at a shiny Smash Hits poster of Suggs. He seems to grin mischievously at her and she smiles gently back at him. Hearing the clatter of crockery in the kitchen below, and wanting to be away from this unhappy house, she thinks about her mates and getting out as soon as possible. Stretching her sleepy arms out from the bed, Snoopy shows ten past nine to her and she rises from a warm candlewick bedspread that has seen better days.

Quietly yawning and rubbing her tired eyes, Shell slowly walks across the room to the window to check out the day. The sun beams down brightly on this spring morning into her teenage bedroom and looking down on to the street below, she watches for a few moments as a growling old green bus passes by with a group of giggling young teens on the top deck. They are passing round a smoke and writing obscenities on the window with black felt tip pen. Shell laughs to herself as it leaves her view and the group of lads run to the back of the bus to pull down their shorts and stick their bare backsides on the grubby glass to moon at the angry car drivers behind.

Heading off to the bathroom with a chuckle, Shell throws water on her face to freshen herself up and quickly brushes her teeth, checking her smile and pouting a kiss in the tiny mirror above the sink.

She sees one of the other kids in the house who gives her an evil stare as she passes.

"Horrible bitch!" She says under her breath. "Gotta get out of here soon."

Wandering back to her little room and her wardrobe covered in her favourite music posters and band stickers, Shell takes out her clothes for the day ahead. One of the stickers peels off slightly as she closes the door. It has Buster Bloodvessel of Bad Manners boldly grinning and sticking out his long tongue at her and she presses it down firmly again with a smile.

Pressing play on her little tape recorder, 'Atomic' By Blondie starts up and she cranks up the volume to the max just to annoy the rest of the household. Dancing across the room with her hairbrush held to her mouth as a microphone, Shell pulls on one of her favourite Fred Perry T-Shirts in burgundy and her two-tone jeans. She feels on top form and brushes her dark brown hair in the dressing table mirror. Terry Hall looks back at her with a badass stare from a tiny black and white picture that is glued to the corner of the flaking glass panel and she blows him a kiss and touches his lips with huge love for her musical idol.

Feeling ready for action and with a quick spray of her favourite Charlie perfume, Shell picks up her beloved tape recorder and stuffs it in her bag. She slings it on to her shoulder and slams the bedroom door as she flies down the stairs at top speed and out on to the street, picking up her pace even more towards the train station.

*****

"Hey suckers!" Shell shouts out teasingly, as she wanders up through the train carriage and finds her gang laughing and play fighting as always.

"Ah my favourite sexy bitch, come to me and sit on my face!" Giggles Giff, in his usual crazy manner. "Where have you been all my life? My bed has been waiting a lifetime for you and your wet lips to touch my cock."

"Oh my fucking good god. He's just unstoppable!" Shell rolls her eyes and kisses his cheek while elbowing him deep in the ribs.

He cowers slightly trying not to show that it hurt a little more than he was expecting but keeps his cool composure to save any embarrassment.

The seats are full with Shell's gang. Daz sits with Lou sharing with her a large box of Milk Tray chocolates that he swiped from the local Bordens corner shop on the way to the station. He stands for a moment and proudly holds up the purple box to all.

"And all because the lady loves Milk Tray." He announces, chuckling to himself and offering Lou first choice from the top layer of chocolates.

Everyone laughs loudly and grabs at the box to take their share.

Tomo and Sam sit together looking through a tatty old newspaper they found on the floor of the train carriage. Both are engrossed in deciding where the cross should go on the 'Spot the Ball' page and arguing over who has the pen first that they had grabbed from Giff's pocket. Tomo smirks widely as he wins the fight for it and as he turns it upside down, the very pretty woman's clothing starts to drain away on the side of the pen revealing her naked figure. He licks the side of it on the pert breasts of the smiling lady. Both of them giggle and Sam snatches it back to redress the completely bare female back into her swimwear.

"Give us me tasty bird back then you fuckin' thieves!" Shouts Giff, snatching his new pen back and making her totally naked again whilst slowly licking the woman's body up and down and winking at Shell.

"Could be you tonight if you play your cards right girl." He says, looking at her seductively and running his hand up between her thighs.

"In your dreams dickhead." She replies coldly, as she rips his hand away from her legs giving him a cold scowl.

Giff shows off his two new Madness badges on his scrap jacket and Shell asks if she can have one.

"Only if you snog me." He sniggers. "They're worth a lot of money they are, you know."

"Yeah right!" Says Shell, full of sarcasm. "Twelve and a half pence from the market they are and two for twenty pence. I saw them last Friday dinner time!"

"Take it or leave it. You'll regret it if you don't." He giggles, licking his lips.

"Think I'll pass dickhead. I'll get my own on Friday and also The Specials one too." Replies Shell, giving him a dig.

"Your loss girl." He says, feeling defeated and sitting back down on to the seat.

Pulling in to the next station, two of the girls from their year at school jump on the train and come to join the gang. Kaz Moreton and Tina Simpson wander in to the carriage looking happy to see the others.

Kaz removes her Walkman from her ears and leaves the headphones hanging round her neck to talk to them all.

"Hey you lot, you off to do some free shoppin' then?" She asks, her tall and slim frame hitting the top of the doorway. She flicks her hand through her short blonde hair and giggles a little at the prospect of shopping together with the others.

"Yeah come and join us. More the merrier!" Says Giff, happily. "I know you two are dab hands at the shops." He chuckles and winks at them making them feel included.

"What ya listening to on your Walkman Kaz?" Asks Giff, curiously.

"Brilliant song 'Love Will Tear Us Apart' By Joy Division." Says Kaz. "Here have a listen."

She hands Giff the headphones and he sits down with her to listen for a moment.

"It's good but it's not 2-Tone so I'll pass." He says removing the headphones. "Not skankin' material that."

Kaz tuts loudly and starts to listen to her music again by herself while watching the day go by out of the carriage window.

Tina stays very quiet with the sultry look on her face that she always silently carries around the school, trying to show her status among the other female teens. One of the top girls for getting the best boys at school but not much of a laugh. Always too busy admiring herself and today is no different. She neatly pats her hair into place and pulls out a tiny mirror from her expensive handbag and checks her appearance, playing with her hair and adding more lipstick to her already covered and glossy lips.

Looking unimpressed, Shell screws up her nose and rolls her eyes wondering why the girl is sitting with *her* mates on *her* Saturday outing.

The train trundles onwards into town. Shell moves away from the two girls and pulls out her own tape recorder from her bag. She looks out of the window to check the progress of the journey and wishes it was heading for her dream place in London, but for now they are bound for the nearby town so she takes out her golden packet of ten Benson & Hedges and puts a cigarette to her lips.

"Who's got a light then you lot?"

The boys leap up and jump on her, tearing the box from her hands to get a smoke and landing on the carriage floor in a heap as she fights them off.

"You only had to ask me for one, arseholes!" She laughs, kicking their backsides while they are down.

Finally lighting her smoke, Shell presses the play button on her tape recorder with a clunk and turns the volume up to max. DJ Tony Blackburn introduces 'Can Can' By Bad Manners on the taped top forty as she jumps around the carriage with her legs high in the air and making the others laugh out loud.

"Do you ever leave that bloody tape recorder at home Shell?" Laughs Kaz.

"No never mate. My music is definitely my life and I never miss a single top forty to record on a Sunday." Replies Shell, continuing to skank up the carriage.

The rest of her mates look up and smile and leap up to join in, twanging braces and singing at the top of their voices for the rest of the journey into town.

*****

Heading out of the station and up through the high street, all eight of them walk eagerly towards the main shopping area. They pass Man at C&A and glance over at the suits all pressed nicely in the window and the smartly dressed manikins all smiling down at them.

"Won't never catch me in a suit and tie." Says Daz, shaking his head and giggling as usual. "No fuckin' way man!"

"Gotta be a tonic suit for me." Replies Giff, nodding at the idea. "Fuckin' smart as hell they are lads. No other one would ever do."

The girls huddle together looking in the window of Chelsea Girl at the latest clothes but quickly catch up with the boys who decide to head straight into Our Price Records to look for some new music.

'Ruder than You' by The Bodysnatchers is blasting in the shop as they enter and all sing along with each other as they dance through the store together.

Giff and Shell head straight for the singles chart. The smell of vinyl makes their hearts beat faster and they all begin to hunt eagerly through the many rows of seven inch singles.

Daz reads the top ten chart list and laughs out loud as 'Making Your Mind Up' by Bucks Fizz stands firm at number one. He tuts loudly and points it out to all of them, making them all giggle along at his findings.

"I'm getting 'Just a Feeling' by Bad Manners." Announces Giff, loudly and proudly. "Still at number fifteen. Top tune!"

"Good shout mate." Replies Tomo.

"Don't you want 'Bermuda Triangle' by Barry Manilow?" Chuckles Daz, pulling his nose longer and jesting about the singer. "Or a bit of Shaky doin' 'This Ole House'" He adds, waving records in the air.

They all giggle at his choices.

He continues to search through the latest chart and does a few Shakin' Stevens dance moves to make all of his friends laugh a little more.

They all giggle at his antics and Shell gives him a dig on the arm.

"Nutter!" She says, eagerly checking through the singles for herself.

"I'm getting 'Grey Day' by Madness" Says Shell, happily strutting up to the till with a record in her hand.

"Have you got a record player now then Shell?" Asks Lou.

"Yeah they got me a second hand shitty one in a sort of suitcase thing for my birthday at the house. It's not got a great sound, the speaker on it is useless but it's all I've got." Says Shell, looking a little grumpy. "I'd rather listen to my cassette player but I do love a bit of vinyl sometimes, ya know."

"Yeah, me too mate. They could've got you a new one. That's just mean." Replies Lou, putting her arm around her friend.

"They bought the other boy there a brand new stack system with tape to tape and everything. Fuckin' mummy's boy hey!" Says Shell, rolling her eyes and turning up her nose."

"Fuck em'." Says Lou, throwing her arms into the air. "They ain't worth even talkin' about."

"Come on you lot let's get goin' to the department store up the road. I need some new make-up and it's the easiest stuff to swipe." Says Kaz, already heading for the door with Tina and looking very excitable.

With their new vinyl safely bought and paid for, the gang follow on. As they quicken their pace up the high street, Daz pulls out a black Clash T-Shirt from under his Harrington jacket. Joe Strummer is rocking it on the front looking extremely cool with the rest of the band and Daz looks very proud of himself as he holds it up against his chest.

"Brilliant. Take a look at that. It was just waitin' for me to have it!" He giggles, hiding it away again back under his clothing.

"You fuckin' scoundrel!" Says Giff, laughing and giving Daz a bear hug as they continue along the high street.

"You can't pass a shop without a challenge mate, can ya?" Giggles Tomo.

"Come on Daz. Time to get me some lippy and eye shadow for West Way. Gotta look me best ya know lads for my Marty." Says Shell, placing her hands on her hips and striking a pose. "Anyway, does anyone wanna gobstopper?"

She pulls out the sweets from her pocket and they all grab into the little white bag like vultures. Each taking a different colour and shoving it into their greedy mouths before heading into the huge department store to try their luck.

The girls all stick together and sheepishly begin to fill their pockets and bags. Unable to see where the boys have gone, they forget about them and concentrate on what they can get themselves and once their pockets are full, they head for the door, trying desperately not to look suspicious but mostly failing miserably.

They begin to split up into two groups. Shell stays with Lou and easily makes it out of the door and on to the street. They up their pace, and hide round the corner in a side street to wait for the others with their hearts beating wildly and giggling madly.

"Oh my God, that was too easy!" Laughs Shell. "Let's stop here and wait for everyone to get out."

Sam ends up walking up to the door with Kaz and Tina. She feels it's not going well as they reach the exit and two big beefy security guards grab a hold of her arm and keep the three of them inside the door.

A third guard arrives and says he believes they have items in their possession that they haven't paid for and marches them upstairs to the office where the police are to be called. Sam looks back to see if she can see her mates but they are nowhere to be seen and realises she's in big trouble.

Meanwhile, Daz, Giff and Tomo have managed to look completely innocent and headed out of the shop to meet the other girls while the coast is clear.

"For fuck's sake! Sam is wrapped up in the shit with those two idiots. We should never have gone anywhere with them!" Tomo says, anxiously. "What the fuck are we gonna do now then?"

"Well, they will be ok I'm sure and we're out of there so why don't we check out our goodies while we wait and see what happens to them." Says Daz, checking his pockets.

"Oh man I've got a bottle of Denim aftershave for the man who doesn't have to try too hard, Brylcream for the Brylcream bounce, an Old Spice soap-on-a-rope, a metal comb, a shaving brush, some Oil of Ulay and a bottle of green apple shampoo!"

"You're the best Daz!" Says Giff, laughing uncontrollably with Tomo. "I'll have a drop of that Oil of Ulay for my beautiful skin."

"Oh man, I've got Cola lip gloss, powder blue eye shadow like Debbie Harry's, black mascara, love heart hair clips and a bottle of Tramp perfume. Not bad for one day's work." Shell chuckles. "Wanted a new eye liner but didn't have the time."

"I only got this." Says Lou, reaching into her pocket. "A bar of Camay soap and a rose scented bath cube! Bit shit really. Didn't get my lip gloss I wanted."

"You got anything Tomo?" Asks Giff.

"Just this." He replies putting his hand down his trousers and pulling out a half full tester bottle of Aramis aftershave and putting a little on his cheeks.

"OOOhh nice one Tom. I'll have a whiff of that mate." Says Giff, grabbing at the little glass bottle.

"We did good you lot." Says Daz, smiling and checking round the corner to see if the girls are anywhere to be seen. "Oh shit, they're being dumped in a police car. I suppose we'd better get off home and leave them to it. Nothing we can do now. Come on let's get back to the train before we get wrapped up in their shit with them."

The five of them tuck away their shopping and head off to the train station with a spring in their step, feeling quite happy with their haul and needing to escape the sights of the security staff.

"Race ya to the train station you lot." Shouts Giff, running ahead of them all. "Last one there buys me a bottle of cider tonight!"

*****

The two of them lay on the bed together giggling in Shell's London home.

"Wow your memory is so good girl." Says Giff, finishing his coffee. "Do you remember what happened to them afterwards? My brain isn't working as well as yours."

"Yeah, the three of them were kept in separate police cells down the station for hours on end. They were more devastated that their parents had to be called!" Shell laughs. "I think they got off with a caution but Sam wasn't allowed out for ages afterwards. I used to sneak up her garden path and chat through the window in the evenings, chucking her a juicy fruit or a few toffos up to her bedroom.

Giff laughs loudly at the thought of the sweets being thrown in to cheer up their friend.

"Kaz said she was petrified in the cell! And Tina, well she just put on her make-up and strutted down the road as if nothing had happened apparently. More concerned that her hair was out of place and she had no lip gloss in the cells."

Both giggle together and Giff splutters on his coffee at the memories. Shell gets up and heads off to the kitchen to make breakfast for them before Giff has to leave for home.

"Hey Shell, one last dance before I have to get going?" Asks Giff, wandering into the lounge with his phone.

He puts on 'Can't Get Used to Losing You' By The Beat and grabs hold of Shell. Losing her balance and dropping the packet of bacon on the kitchen floor, she swings round to dance with her mate and both sing together with their arms round one another.

"Hey, I text Lou and she's gonna contact everyone for an evening at her place and I'm coming down for it. We'll call it our memory night." Says Shell, with a huge grin. "Hoping it will be next week. Plenty of food and drinks and loads of chats about the old days."

"Yeah, that'll be just right. I'm definitely up for that!" Replies Giff, holding her tightly as they sway to the music. "Just what a set of oldies like us will need to brighten our week."

"Thanks for the beautiful dance and the special memories boy but the fuckin' sausages are burning!!"

Chapter 4

After a week of thinking about everyone and feeling her life is going totally off track, it's finally Friday afternoon and Shell has been driving for nearly two hours. She heads towards her old hometown by the sea ready for a night with all her best mates at Lou's place.

'Wooly Bully' By Bad Manners blasts out of her car stereo and Shell sings along at the top of her voice, smiling as she moves to the music in her driving seat.

Full of anticipation and excitement, she passes the landmark windmill on the hill and the old church steeple stares back at her as the memories start to return again. She thinks about how the town pulls her back every time to her old friends and how she broke away for so many years, only to now be back in the heart of it all.

Taking a sharp turn and pulling into Lou's road, she puts on her handbrake and looks around at the area she remembers so well with both a touch of happiness and a hint of sadness at the life she left behind there.

The music stops abruptly as she stops the engine and slamming the car door, Shell sprays a little perfume to her wrists and neatens her hair. She looks down at her cherry red boots and checks her fishnet stockings. Smiling to herself, she eagerly heads down the path to the front door and rings the doorbell.

The door opens immediately with all of her friends jumping about excitedly like young teens again and hugging her tightly.

"Come in darlin' we're ready for action in here!" Giggles Lou.

"Oh man, this is so good." Says Shell, taking a huge glass of wine from Lou's hand. I've missed you all so much. Me and Giff had the best night together last week at mine, didn't we mate?"

"Yeah top night darlin'." Says Giff, kissing her cheek.

"Come on you lot, let's get smashed and talk shit all night!" Says Daz, giggling.

"Of course mate. Can't think of anywhere I'd rather be." Says Shell, throwing her jacket on to the stairs. "Great to see all your Fred Perry shirts and Doc Martens out for the night you lot!"

"Marty's here Shell." Whispers Lou, softly. "You gonna be ok?"

Shell freezes for a moment then nods her head as she swallows hard and prepares to enter the room.

"Lou has made enough food for an army." Says Shell, laughing at the huge spread on the table.

"It's so good though." Replies Giff, taking another cocktail sausage on a stick and shoving it in to his mouth along with a slice of mustard covered pork pie.

"I tried to put in as much of the seventies and eighties food as I could remember." Says Lou, showing them the piled up selection. "Sandwich spread, French fancies, Angel delight, dairylea, and look a huge Bird's trifle as my centre piece amongst other things."

"Oh wow Lou, you have done us proud girl." Says Shell, giving her mate a kiss on the cheek. "I can't wait to get stuck in to this lot!"

She looks across the room and gives a slight smile of acknowledgement to Marty as she takes a triangle shaped lemon curd sandwich for herself and gulps a large glass of wine to calm her nerves.

*****

'Ghost town' by The Specials plays in the background and as the drinks flow and the memories become more explicit, Giff stands up to raise a glass.

"To the bestest days of our lives and to my bestest mates always!" He says, happily slurring and slightly wobbling.

The room becomes full of laughter and clanking glasses as they all raise their own glasses and say cheers in unison.

"I've got this top idea for the rest of the evening." He says, with a naughty grin. "Truth or dare! Remember playing that? Let's do it now for a laugh."

The giggling becomes louder and it's agreed.

"Ok, ok, I'll start this then." He says, taking control of the night. "I'll start from my left side and we'll go in turn from there. Shell, you're first."

"Oh shit! Why me? She exclaims, taking another rather large gulp of wine.

"Truth or dare mate?"

"Dare." She says hesitantly.

"Ok, I dare you to go and snog the love of your life over there. I know it's what you both want and really can't keep your hands off each other so I dare you to let go of everything that is stopping you and snog the arse off him!" Shell clears her throat and looks across the room at Marty with an apprehensive but loving grin on her face.

Both smile at each other knowing this will happen and Shell hesitantly walks over to him amid loud applause from the others. She sits comfortably on his lap and looks straight at his waiting gaze. Taking his head in her hands she softly starts to kiss her beautiful man. The memories start to flood back of all they have been through and meeting up again in the hotel. Now all that has been said about just being friends seems insignificant and the strong feelings still remain for them both.

"Well, that's all going to plan then." Laughs Giff, with a cheeky look on his face.

The others look pleased at the sight of the kiss and wait patiently for it to end.

"Still love you boy." Says Shell, stroking his cheek as she gets up and heads back to her chair blushing a little but smiling heavily.

"My turn." Says Shell, standing up again. "Come on Giff, truth or dare?"

"Ha, truth." He says, in an unconcerned voice.

"Ok, with all the bravado you give us, is there truthfully anyone in this room that you actually got off with at school?"

He looks a little sheepish and giggles slightly.

"Well ok. Yeah there is." He says as he looks across the room. "Me and Lou once did it up against the wall in the grubby old toilets of the underground car park after you'd all gone home."

Lou puts her head in her hands and giggles with embarrassment.

"Oh my fuckin' god." She says, shaking her head.

"We'd had quite a bit of cider and were just fuckin' about and ended up snoggin' and the rest as they is history!" Laughs Giff.

"And you never told any of us!" Says Daz, spluttering into his beer.

"It was a teenage drunken escapade and we've never spoken about it since." Laughs Lou, going over and kissing him on the cheek. "Dickhead!" She says, being very giggly and looking rather pink in the cheeks.

"How was it then Lou?" Laughs Sam.

"It was the best she's ever had of course." Replies Giff, standing up and punching the air before she can get a word in edgeways. "I am the boss of 1981."

Lou shakes her head as she curls up into an embarrassed ball on the sofa and the rest laugh very loudly.

'Walking in the Sunshine' by Bad Manners plays in the background and the girls all get up and dance along with their drinks in hand feeling like they are back in time.

"I'm asking this time round." Says Lou, still blushing from Giff's truth. "Marty, your turn. Truth or dare darlin'?"

"Oh fuck!" He says, thinking hard. "Truth I guess."

"Ok Marty, What other girl did you fancy at school? There must have been others. Come on who else did it for you?"

Marty looks at Shell, raising his eyebrow and looking rather uncomfortable. He turns his gaze towards Lou and smiles awkwardly.

"For fuck's sake, well, I suppose I did fancy Tina Simpson a bit. She was good looking but I would never have acted on it." He replies, screwing his face up a little.

"Fuckin' Tina Simpson, no way! You're so shallow!" Laughs Shell, feeling a hint of jealousy raging up inside her. "Well, I beat off that competition then. She was the top girl. All the boys fancied her!"

Shell stands up and strikes a pose proudly.

"Up yours! Tina fuckin' Simpson." She declares with a pout. "You're all fuckin' shallow you men!"

The room becomes raucous with laughter and Marty breathes a sigh of relief that his turn is over.

"I'll ask this time." Says Marty, standing up.

"Daz, truth or dare?"

"Oh fuck, here we go. I'll go dare." He says, reluctantly. "And I know exactly what is coming you fuckhead!"

Marty starts to laugh and pats Daz on the shoulder.

"Ok, I dare you to sit and tell the rest of them about what happened during the twelve hour sponsored dance in 1981 down the community centre."

"Oh bloody hell yeah." Says Shell, butting in. "It was from 10 o'clock on a Saturday morning. I remember it well and I can recall vividly the lead up to it on the Friday before too. What happened to me and Lou at school that day sticks in my head." Adds Shell, desperate to tell all. "Come on Daz let's relive our memories. I'm dying to know why you disappeared that day!"

"He most definitely *did* disappear that day." Says Marty, giggling to himself. "And I know exactly why so off you go Daz."

"Well how about I start Daz and recall my Friday dramas for a few laughs then you can finish it and reveal where you went." Says Shell, excitedly.

"I know you were fuckin' hammered mate!" Laughs Giff. "I can't wait to get to the bottom of this one!"

"Oh man!" Daz starts to laugh and begins to go rather red in the face. "Go on Shell you go for it as your memory is better than mine and I will tell you all the stupid little secret that me and Marty have kept all these years.

"Well, here goes." Says Shell, taking a large mouthful of wine and picking up a pickled onion. "Are you sitting comfortably? Then we'll begin."

*****

1981

"Oh for fuck's sake!" Says Shell, under her breath as she storms out of D3 with another detention hanging over her head. "Can't believe I've been rumbled. She's a sour faced bitch that Deeson. I hate her with a vengeance and wanna give her a slap on her wobbly neck!"

She slams the door with rage and finds Lou and Daz waiting patiently outside for her.

"You ok Shell? What's happened?" Asks Daz, curiously. "What's the saggy old bat done today?"

"Come on, what the fuck is it this time mate?" Asks Lou, adjusting her tiny school tie that has been the fashion this year with the girls. All three inches of it flattened down into a miniature replica and the rest of it tucked in between the buttons of her tight white shirt.

"Been fuckin' sussed out for forging my foster carer's signature on seven sick notes!" Shell replies, with a mischievous chuckle. "Detention tonight! A hundred lines of 'I will not lie to my teacher ever again' Ha!" She laughs again with Lou and links arms with her two mates.

"Ah, you're so funny girl." Says Daz, giggling madly. "Got away with six of them before Deeson caught on to it then, hey? Fair play to ya my friend, that's pretty good going!"

"Come on, let's go for a smoke." Says Lou, pulling out something from her pocket. "Here you are, I've got cola cubes mate, have one."

Shell takes the little square of sugar coated delight from the white paper bag.

"What *you* gonna be doin' Daz?" Asks Shell.

"I'm comin' wiv ya both." He says excitedly. "Not leavin' me behind when you're havin' a smoke, bitches. I'll squat on to the top of the loo in case anyone comes in."

The three of them giggling in a huddle, begin to head off rebelliously into D block toilets and enter a very tightly fitting cubicle together. Shell pulls out her small black box of ten John Player Special and they strike a match, lighting one up to share in the tiny room.

Daz clambers up on to the top of the toilet and crouches down, trying not to laugh too loudly with his feet sitting precariously, one on each side of the open toilet pan.

"Comfy Daz?" Asks Lou with a chuckle.

Daz tries to hold in his belly laugh as he becomes a little red in the face.

"Fuck em'" Says Shell, inhaling deeply and blowing smoke down the toilet pan between Daz's legs. "Won't be goin' to that." She says, casually. "They can shove it up their arse. We've got our twelve hour sponsored dance tomorrow morning at the community centre and I've got to get myself ready tonight. I can't bloody wait. Skankin' it up with the lads for a whole twelve hours! Total heaven!"

Lou pulls out a copy of Look-in magazine that has Bad Manners on the front and they all take a look at what's inside.

"Yeah gonna be a brilliant laugh there. Where we meeting then? And what's Sam and the boys doin'?" Asks Lou, taking a drag of her cigarette and quickly waving the smoke away from the top of the cubicle.

Before Shell can answer, footsteps can be heard through the squeaky main door and she drops her smoke into the toilet bowl and quickly flushes it away before shoving polo mints into their mouths and giggling frantically.

Lou shoves her magazine back into her bag and tries to be silent as they begin to giggle under their breath.

"Don't make me laugh." Whispers Daz, now with tears in his eyes from holding in his belly laugh.

"Whoever is in that cubicle smoking, come out right this minute!" Says the stern voice of miserable Miss Fearful.

The girls roll their eyes, spit out the last of their polo mints and sheepishly open the door, awaiting the wrath of the detestable and nasty, head of girls PE.

Daz stays perched silently on the toilet as the girls pull the door closed behind them to hide him.

"Get your disgraceful little bodies down to the sports hall right now." She bellows. Her spiky black hair standing to attention and her saggy, wrinkled cheeks shaking with anger.

"You are supposed to be doing badminton I believe but now you will go and get changed into your PE kits and get yourselves on to the school field. I will be following you, just mark my words and you will both run around the whole field ten times before the end of school, without stopping. Now get out of here and move it!" She spits slightly in her shouting rage as she makes her demands and Shell wipes away a drop her dank saliva that has landed on her cheek and gags at the smell of her rancid breath.

Lou and Shell give her an evil stare as they pass her stern and angry face and stay strong together, linking arms like solid allies.

Every girl in the school despises Fearful. Known as the water witch for her evil ways of making the teens get completely naked in the mould ridden, ancient shower block and marching them through in a regimented line for a minimum stand in time of ten long minutes. The girls always cower in the cold while the miserable sergeant major like woman, struts up and down examining their progress.

Lou and Shell tut and roll their eyes as they head off towards the changing rooms of the PE block.

"Ah for fuck's sake you two." Says Daz, tapping them on the shoulder from behind and giggling. "Can't even manage a smoke without getting done!"

The three of them laugh together and wander down the main path feeling stronger together.

"Thanks for coverin' for me girls. I'll see ya after school you two, I'm fuckin' off. Hate PE and not doin' it. Goin' over the fence. Enjoy your run!" He says, jogging off towards the exit.

"See ya Daz. Catch ya later." They both shout. "You should be doin' this for us after we covered for ya!"

Daz giggles and waves as he scarpers across the school field.

"Cheeky git!" Shouts Lou as he goes.

In the changing room, they take out their kit from their drawstring bags and put on black stretchy shorts, red Trutex T-Shirts and black slip-on plimsolls.

"I fuckin' hate PE *and* that bitch." Says Shell, angrily. Can't wait to leave this school and run away to somewhere new where these miserable fucked up teachers can't touch me!"

"Yeah fuckin' Fearful is an evil witch and needs takin' off her broomstick and drowning in her deep black cauldron!" Replies Lou.

They both snigger at the thought of her fighting for breath in a huge fired up pot, getting her comeuppance for all she has put them through in their years at the school.

The outraged girls head out on to the field and begin their painfully long run. Some of the boys from their year are in the middle of a football match and stop to wolf-whistle as the two of them pass with shouts of 'Get your kit off for the lads' and 'nice legs, shame about the face'.

"Fuck off you lot." Shouts Lou, sticking two fingers up at the crowd of sweaty teenage boys.

"Yeah, up yours! Go shove your tiny dicks up your arses!" Adds Shell, as she lifts her Trutex top and flashes her teen white bra at them.

"In your dreams wankers!" She bawls, and both bend over with a stitch in their bellies from laughing too much and get on their way.

*****

As their task is completed, the girls try to catch their breath and wander slowly into the changing rooms exhausted and heavily throw themselves down on the bench.

"There's no way I'm doin' any detention tonight Lou. I'm outta here, we've got twelve hours of skankin' to get ready for tomorrow." Says Shell, very quietly so that the water witch can't hear.

"No one leaves here until they have showered PROPERLY!" Demands the stern voice of Fearful. "All clothing off and line up along the shower wall. You have ten seconds, now move it!"

"Ten….. Nine….. Eight….. Seven….. Six….. Anyone not there will very much regret it! Five….. Four….. Three….. Two…… One….. Right, walk in a straight line through the showers and WASH! No talking, off you go and I'm watching every move you make!"

"Yeah course you are you fucked up pervert!" Sniggers Shell. "We've been in here for ten minutes now for sure. I'm bloody freezin' my tits off!"

All the girls giggle quietly at her comment as they stand in line waiting for their nightmare to end.

"Right, walk through the showers and out the other end and get dressed. Two minutes to walk right through and counting!" The witch continues.

"Oh man I'm outta here." Says Shell.

"Me too. Come on we gotta get past Deeson's office yet. She'll be on ya for this detention for sure!" Replies Lou. Quickly getting dressed and grabbing their things together, the two girls get out of the PE block sharpish and decide to do as Daz did earlier and avoid the office by running across the field to the back of the school and on to the building site where the gang often meet up.

Out of breath but very happy to be away, the girls see Giff and Tomo jumping about on a pile of bricks and Daz and Sam on the huge grey pipes, eating some goodies out of a large square tin.

"Hey what ya got you lot?" Shouts Shell, getting her breath back. "And where have you been Sam? Couldn't find you all day."

"Making these!" Replies Sam, licking chocolate cream off her fingers.

"I've been in D3, got caught forging sick notes!" Says Shell, huffing to herself.

They all giggle at Shell's misfortune.

"Ah mate come and eat my cakes with us." Says Sam, kindly offering her old red tin with ROVER biscuits written on the side. Her mum had once bought the biscuits for a Christmas treat a couple of years back and kept the empty tin for any homemade cakes.

"Chocolate butterfly cakes, made 'em in cookery today." She says, stuffing another into her mouth.

Giff and Tomo both have their mouths bursting with chocolate cream and can barely speak. Their eyes rolling into the back of their heads with the heavenly taste.

"Give us one then." Says Shell, eagerly.

"And me!" Adds Lou. "What's the plan for tomorrow then you lot?"

Shell pulls out her tape recorder and presses the play button. 'One Step Beyond' by Madness blares out and the little speaker struggles hard to keep up.

The boys all leap up from what they are doing and skank madly for the duration of the song making the girls giggle together.

As the song ends, Giff wipes his forehead after the crazy dancing and catches his breath a little to get a few words out.

"Meet at the bandstand behind the community centre." He says, with more cake crumbs dropping from his lips and shoving in the last of the chocolate cream. "Starts at ten so meet about quarter to and we'll get in there and skank it up! Make sure you bring some booze from somewhere it will be a laugh being smashed by midday!"

"Well, you all know by now that I'll have my jacket full of goodies!" Giggles Daz.

They all laugh and agree as they jump off the pipes. Sam closes the lid of the tin and notes to herself that there are none left to take home as she does so.

"See ya tomorrow then you lot." Shouts Giff, getting on his bike and riding off with Tomo closely following behind.

"See ya later girls." Says Shell, heading off home to prepare herself for tomorrow. "Grange Hill is on so it's time to get home to watch that gorgeous Tucker Jenkins!"

"I'm there too." Shouts Sam, giggling. "He's a bit of alright!"

"Me Too. Catch ya tomorrow girls." Shouts Lou, raising her hand to wave behind her.

The gang all head off in different directions feeling a wave of excitement for the weekend ahead of them.

*****

Four greasy rockers have taken over the bandstand blasting 'Highway to Hell' by AC/DC on their tape recorder when Shell arrives and she screws up her face a little at the sight of them with their long hair and dirty denim jackets covered in patches of their favourite bands.

She heads off across to the cliffs on the seafront and waits on the old wooden bench. She stares over at the sea rippling small waves on the rocks and looks up at the old landmark lighthouse, wondering if life would be better living alone up inside of it instead of being in foster care.

If I was up there, no one would ever bother me, she thinks to herself. *Never have to deal with an unloving family ever again*. She reaches into her pocket and pulls out a bag of sweets and looks through the assortment of penny chews, deciding on a bazooka Joe gum. She looks at the little comic strip inside as a hand appears over her shoulder stealing a sweet from the bag.

"Unlucky sexy bitch it's all mine!" Shouts Giff, Running round in circles with Tomo behind.

"Arsehole!" Shouts Shell, pulling away her little bag and taking out her favourite pink shrimp to hide for herself for later. "Here Tomo." She says, offering it over to him.

He dips his hand in and pulls out a chocolate tool.

"Cheers mate." He says, joining her on the bench. "Chocolate spanner, my favourite!"

Shell smiles at the arrival of them both as it takes away her thoughts and blocks out her worries.

Lou and Sam arrive together and look excited for the day ahead. Sam has a new mini skirt and loafers and is happily showing them off to the rest of the gang.

"Here girls, wanna sweet?" Offers Shell.

Sam pulls out a black jack and Lou a golf ball gum.

"Loving the new loafers Sam. Where did ya get em' from?" Asks Shell.

"Friday market in town. Love em' hey!" She replies, smiling sweetly at her purchase.

"Anyone got any alcohol for later then?" Asks Shell. "All I've got is a can of Top Deck Shandy for fuck's sake! Ain't gonna get me far."

"I've got a Snowball and a Babycham out of Dad's bar." Replies Lou, giggling.

"Well, I've got a half bottle of Bacardi!" Exclaims Sam, taking it out of her bag and waving it in the air.

"Gonna have to nick some of yours coz me mum was in and I couldn't get anything." Says Giff, in a bit of a huff.

"Well, I've got six cans of Skol so we're alright for later." Adds Tomo. "Keep it all tucked away in ya bags and we can do it during the breaks. I think you get a ten minute break every hour."

"HEYYY WANKERS never fear Daz is here!" He shouts, throwing down his heavy bag on arrival.

"What the hell you got in there boy?" Asks Giff, trying to open it to see the contents of the bag.

Daz whips it away and opens it for himself.

"Well, as always I am the bearer of amazing goodies." He announces, smugly. "Firstly I have two packs of golden wonder cheese and onion. I have a Banjo, a packet of peanut treets, some frazzles, a packet of strawberry jelly and a box of jam tarts." He pauses for breath. "Oh and forty Rothmans, a bottle of Cherry Brandy, half a bottle of Martini and some chocolate liqueurs!"

The rest of them fall around laughing at Daz's stash for the day.

"Brilliant Daz." Says Shell, giving him a hug. "Gotta try and hide that lot then. It's time to go in and get skankin'."

Grabbing their bags and feeling a rush of excitement, the gang head for the entrance of the centre.

The old pale blue building looks shabby and run down as they enter. The main hall smells damp and mouldy and the tired painted walls have seen better days.

The mass of young teens find their own space to occupy and throw down their bags. Small pockets of friends stick together feeling confident with their peers and prepare themselves for the long dancing task ahead.

Pete gives the gang a wave from behind his disco and the light boxes start to flash as he prepares to start along with a huge blast from the smoke machine.

"Twelve hours dancing then you lot with a ten minute break every hour. Let's do this!" Shouts Pete, starting the first track of the day with 'Stomp!' By The Brothers Johnson.

The hall explodes with cheers from excited dancers ready to keep going for the full twelve hours and hoping to hear their favourite sounds as they go.

Shell, Sam and Lou dance in a little circle and Sam pulls out her little bottle of Bacardi from the waist of her tight jeans.

"Ha, you bought it in with ya. Bad girl." Laughs Shell. "Give us a swig then?"

"And me." Giggles Lou, getting closer to the girls for a hideout.

The three of them craftily take a gulp of neat Bacardi each and grimace at the taste of it making their eyes water.

It makes them a little red in the face and goes straight to their heads.

Being extremely giggly, they hear Pete the DJ on the microphone.

"This one's for the skankin' girls over there in the corner waiting for a top tune." He shouts and gives the girls a wink as 'Tears of a Clown' by The Beat blasts out of the huge black boxes of speakers.

The girls cheer and run through the centre of the dancefloor leaping up and down as Shell blows a kiss to the DJ behind his deck.

Giff and Tomo run in to the centre along with the girls and the five of them happily get skankin' together loving every moment. The boys braces hanging low and bouncing around as they dance with four sets of Doc Martens and a pair of brand new loafers gleaming. The five of them get amongst it on the dance floor singing at the top of their voices.

*****

A few hours into the dance and the hall is steaming with sweaty teens dancing to 'Rappers Delight' by The Sugarhill Gang. Pete decides it's time to calm it all down for a bit and as the ten minute break arrives, he puts on 'Total Eclipse of the Heart' by Bonnie Tyler. The gang head for the door on their short time out, looking very hot and tired and completely disinterested in the smoochy song being pumped out right now.

"Oh man I'm fucked!" Says Giff, pulling his braces back off his shoulders and letting them hang loose down the sides of his jeans.

"Me too!" Replies Tomo, wiping his forehead on the sleeve of his beloved Ben Sherman shirt.

Daz pulls out his packet of Rothmans and passes them all round to his mates.

"Nice one Daz." Says Shell, perching on a bench between the trees to camouflage herself.

"Fuckin' hell, dunno how much more I can do in there man!" Says Daz, taking the first long pull on his cigarette and sweating profusely.

Tomo pulls out some cans of Skol and gives one to Daz.

"Here ya go mate, that'll cool ya down." He says, kindly.

"Nice one Tom." He replies, slurring his words a little. Quickly pulling the can ring, he downs most of it in one go.

"Bloody hell Daz, you've already done a bottle of Cherry Brandy and half of that Martini you bought with you." Says Shell, giggling with him. "And you've spent most of the time out here ya bloody cheat!"

"Oh I'm ok." He says, laying down on the grass and laughing his head off at absolutely nothing. "Just give me ten minutes and I'll sneak back in."

They all look at one other and roll their eyes a little as they all finish their smokes and head back inside leaving Daz in the long grass to sober up a bit, hidden by the bushes.

Pete is kicking off the next hour with 'Cool for Cats' by Squeeze and Shell and her friends leap across the dance floor together enjoying every moment. The girls get deeply into their dancing and totally forget about a very smashed Daz laying outside in the long grass.

*****

Marty Clark is finishing work and desperate to get down to see his girl at the community centre. He jumps into his beloved Mark 2 Ford Escort, cranks up his UB40 tape with 'One in Ten' and drives through town and into the main car park.

Stopping his two furry dice from swinging on the mirror he checks his appearance and slicks back his thick dark hair before jumping out of the driver's seat and over to the centre doors.

He can hear the Pete's music blasting as he gets near to the main entrance. 'Dance Yourself Dizzy' By Liquid gold is echoing through the walls and the sound of teens laughing and singing along makes him chuckle a little.

Waiting outside for Shell's next ten minute break, he wanders over to the trees to have a smoke and pulls out a cigarette from his box. As he lights up, he hears some strange grunting and groaning noises along with girls giggling behind him.

Being extremely curious, he looks into the bushes only to find a half-naked Daz getting a hand job from Mandy Jessop and on the other side of him is the horror from school, Stinky Stockwell, with one of her huge sweaty breasts shoved into his mouth.

"Fuckin' hell Daz, you're lowering yourself today boy." He says, laughing at the sight before him. "What the fuck are you doing?"

Daz looks up, bleary eyed and looking slightly bewildered. "Where am I?" He asks. "Where's me trousers?"

Mandy quickly removes her knickers from the top of Daz's head and Stockwell jumps off, putting her pale and veiny lump of a bosom back into a very discoloured, grubby old vest.

Marty sees that Daz's nipples have a blackcurrant jam tart stuck on each one and feels pretty lost for words.

The two girls pick up the half empty box of jam tarts and the open pack of strawberry jelly and stand up with evil looks on their faces.

"What's it gotta do with you anyway shithead?" Asks Mandy, putting her pants back on. "You're just fuckin' jealous, arsehole!"

"Where's the dosh then that you promised?" Asks Stockwell, standing with her hands on her hips and glaring at Daz. "A quid each you said for our services. Don't give ya all that attention for free ya know! Come on, cough up the cash."

"Fuck off both of you, ya dirty bitches." Shouts Marty, helping Daz up off the ground. "Come on mate, I'll get you in the car and take you home."

Daz stands up wobbling slightly and lumps of strawberry jelly fall from his groin area along with the two jam tarts falling to the ground leaving a sticky mess on his chest. Pulling down his T-shirt, he looks a little embarrassed and he pulls up his jeans, straightening himself up and staggers along with Marty's help.

Marty huffs a little to himself not being able to see his girl but begrudgingly helps him to the car. Just as he goes to open the back door for him, suddenly Daz looks rather green and turns to the side, vomiting violently on to the grounds of the car park.

"Fuck me, man! Good job you did that before getting into my motor or you'd be scrubbing it all weekend!"

"Where's me liqueurs gone?" Slurs Daz. "And me strawberry jelly?"

"Get in the car ya dickhead, you ain't gonna need liqueurs in your state." He sniggers. "And I won't breathe a word to the others about Jessop and Stockwell if you behave yourself!"

Marty rolls his eyes, slicks back his thick black hair in the mirror and turns up his cassette player blasting out 'I Think It's Going to Rain Today' by UB40 as he drives off through the town.

"Oh man I feel like shit!" Says Daz, falling deeply into the back seat of Marty's car and feeling extremely embarrassed. "Was that really Stinky Stockwell I was with?"

"Yeah you've pulled big time mate! Real hot stinky stuff!" Marty laughs out loud. "I think you've hit an all-time low there mate!!"

"Oh fuckin' bollocks." Replies Daz, burying his head into the back seat.

*****

Daz and Shell have a hug together after finishing their story. "I only know most of it because Marty told me the details." Says Daz with his face in his hands. "I've got very little recollection of that afternoon but I've got to say that I am pretty happy about the memory loss!"

"NO WAY DAZ!! All these years and you never told a soul about Mandy Jessop and Stinky Stockwell!!" Shouts Lou. "What the fuck were you thinking? You dickhead!"

Daz shrugs his shoulders. "Fuck knows!" He shakes his head awkwardly.

By now all the others are on the floor, their bellies hurting with laughter.

'Up the Junction' by Squeeze is playing in the background much to their delight.

"This is something else tonight you lot." Says Giff. "Brilliant! No wonder he never told anyone. I'd be hiding that one too!"

"We all wondered why and how you got home that day and now we know." Laughs Shell.

"I was completely hammered on the Cherry Brandy." Replies Daz. "Never touch that stuff ever again! Anyway, that's enough of that. You've all had your good laugh at my expense. I'm asking this time."

He takes a prawn vol-au-vent and shoves it in his mouth before taking his turn.

"Sam, truth or dare?" He splutters, his mouth still full of pastry.

"Oh God, ok I'll go truth."

"Ok, right then, tell the truth. First ever snog. EVER! I bet you've never told us about it." Says Daz, with a naughty chuckle.

Daz sits down again, extremely happy to be out of the spotlight and takes a long deep breath in relief.

"Ok here goes. I actually snogged Gatesy behind the bike sheds." She says, quickly putting her head in to her hands.

"He came on to me one lunch time over the field and I thought I'd have a quick go."

"We walked over to the bike sheds together and had a bit of a go of it." She continues.

"No way!" Bellows Shell. "You snogged my Gatesy! Uuh! Devastated!"

"Sorry Shell. He was a bit of a looker though and I couldn't look a gift horse in the mouth." Sam giggles and gives her mate a hug.

"And there was me thinking he just wasn't interested in girls back then but turns out he just wasn't interested in *me*!" Replies Shell, hitting her forehead with the palm of her hand and falling backwards on to the sofa.

"Was it fantastic Sam?" Asks Shell, hesitantly. "Oh man, I so wanted to do that back then. I dreamed of that happening to me every night!"

"Just bloody stupid kids fumbling and messing around mate. Nothing amazing I can give you my word on that." Sam assures her friend.

"That's a relief! I'll definitely sleep better now." Laughs Shell. Quickly moving on, Sam gets ready to ask someone else. She takes a cheese and pineapple cocktail stick and smiles. 'Police and Thieves' by Junior Murvin is playing and she sways to the sound as she begins her turn.

"Tomo, truth or dare darlin'?"

"Oh no, here we go again." Says Tomo, slightly cowering in the corner.

"Go on then, truth."

"Ok, tell us all the truth about your first experience of any kind with a girl." Says Sam, quizzingly. "What did you get up to?"

"Oh shit yeah, I remember it well." He says, smiling. "Well, I was over the field at school. It was a lunch time I think. There was a big gang of us all fuckin' about but I can't recall all of them. Think you were there Giff as we were always together but when you all left, it was just me and Kaz Moreton. It was really awkward but I remember she was totally gagging for it. She gave me two Benson and Hedges and a sherbet dip dab to kiss her!"

They all begin to laugh out loud and Shell splutters her wine as she takes a sip listening to the story.

"Anyway, I did as she asked and ended up putting my hand inside her bra and feeling for her nipples and then fingering her on the grass! I was quite proud of myself afterwards and the dip dab certainly tasted better after that!" He giggles madly.

The room is filled with applause.

"Oh man this has been the best laugh." Says Shell. "Let's have some more music and dancing. I can't take no more, my face hurts from laughing."

Lou cranks up 'Uptown Top Rankin' by Althea and Donna and the room erupts with dancing and singing late into the night.

"Sod the neighbours!" Shouts Lou, swaying round the floor with a huge smile on her face and glowing from the wine.

*****

"Hey, we're doing well you lot." Says Shell, glugging on her wine glass. "It's quarter past one and the oldies are all still up!"

She glances over at Marty dancing and smiles at him sweetly. 'Don't Stand So Close To Me' by The Police starts to play and Shell makes her way over to him.

"Hey, you ok?" She asks, wrapping her arms around his neck.

"I am now!" He replies softly, holding her close to him. "How do we keep ending up like this?"

"I'm not sure but I guess we have a solid bond that keeps bringing us back together."

"Shall we do a few more truth or dares before we finish up tonight?" Asks Giff, with a cheeky grin and tapping hiss glass for everyone's attention. "I'm sure there's a few we haven't done."

"Go on then Giff, you go boy." Says Shell, letting go of Marty and slouching down on to the sofa.

"Couple more then we're off." Says Tomo, looking very drunk and exhausted.

"Shell, truth or dare?" Asks Giff, winking at her.

"Course it's gonna be me!" She says, huffing and puffing. "Truth then."

"Tell us your truth then Shell. Who was your first experience of boys with?"

"Well, that's an easy one." She says, sitting upright on the sofa. "Gatesy was the one I first fell head over heels for but much to my sadness, I never got him."

The room is filled with 'ahh' and 'ooh' as they all listen and she continues.

"I did kiss Andy Lovelock behind the West Way disco one night in the bushes when I was twelve though. It was very sloppy and messy and I hated it. If that was what kissing was going to be like then I was already done with it. And he had rotten breath that tasted like soup and made me gag."

The room is filled with laughter as they think about his soupy smell.

"Oxtail or tomato Shell?" Giggles Lou.

"Fuckin' Andy Lovelock!" Exclaims Marty. "What were you thinkin' girl? He was a minging boy and all covered in spots!" He laughs out loud.

"He was the only one who asked me to smooch at the disco back then so I went with it and danced with him to 'If You Leave Me Now' by Chicago. And he bloody well couldn't do a smooch dance to save his life. He kept standing on my feet and kneeing me where it hurts!" She giggles. "It wasn't the best start to my teenage male experience. I was ready to give up after that!"

"I haven't seen him for years, no idea what ever happened to him." Says Daz. "Probably sitting by the tube station waiting for you to return after all these years in London Shell!"

They all laugh together at the thought of Shell and Andy smooching.

"Ok, last one coz we're all fucked and need some kip." Says Giff. "So, to end this amazing evening of memories and friendship, truth or dare Marty?"

"Fuckin' hell, why me?" He laughs, putting his head in his hands. "Dare."

"I'm going to put on a slow song from West Way days and I dare you to do a full smooch with Shell as she only got one with Lovelock back then."

"Oh man." He says, looking at Shell for her reaction. "Come on then darlin' let's do this and give them what they want."

"Now this one is what I always remember Pete rolling out at the end of most of the West Way disco nights so here ya go." Smiles Giff, and he puts on 'Please Don't Go' by KC and the Sunshine Band.

Both Marty and Shell smile at each other and in their heads they both begin to relive the memory of their last night together at his house. Laid on his mum's sofa in that blue sleeping bag, Marty thought he didn't have a care in the world that night.

The two of them take one another in their arms. Slowly dancing together at the side of the dining table, as far away from the others as they can manage.

Marty kisses her forehead softly as the music plays and their friends look on, feeling the love between them.

"I'll always love you no matter what but I have to say, I most definitely did smooch with you at the West Way so never say I didn't." He whispers quietly and holds her very tightly until the end of the song.

"I'm sorry I've been ignoring you and hiding away. It's been a tough few months for me." Says Marty, kissing her again.

"I've missed you ya know."

"I've missed you too." She replies, as she finishes the dance. They all stand and applaud as the two of them part.

"Now let's get all that shit off and end on something decent." Laughs Giff, and he quickly changes the tempo of the night with 'Guns of Navarone.' By The Specials, getting the whole gang to skank wildly together before ending their night of memories.

As the track starts, the whole room goes crazy with them all up dancing together and the night is ended with the best sounds to remember it by.

The friends all look exhausted but happy after their top night and begin to say their goodbyes and all slowly head off after an evening filled with love and friendship.

"Don't forget I have our London night booked in a couple of weeks for The Specials. It's gonna be amazing you lot." Says Lou, hugging them all. "Thanks so much for coming you lot. It's been the best time."

Shell lays on Lou's sofa to sleep off the wine before she has to drive back to London in the morning. Her head still full of confusion.

Lou kisses her forehead and leaves her to rest.

"Goodnight my darling friend. Love you always." Says Lou, blowing a kiss from the hallway door. "Sleep well."

"Night mate. Thanks for always being there. Love you too."

Chapter 5

A little worse for wear from the night of alcohol and crazy memories, Shell wakes with a sore neck and a very stiff back. She lifts herself up from Lou's sofa and rubs her eyes. Grabbing a large glass of water from the kitchen, she turns on some music very low and stands at the window staring at all the different birds feeding from their own little table in the middle of the garden and remembering the laughs they all had last night. The sight in the garden feels apt as 'Three Little Birds' by Bob Marley plays from Lou's portable radio on the shelf.

Her focus seems fixed on Marty and that kiss. That feeling in the pit of her stomach that just won't go away, still eating away at her heart after so long.

Downing the rest of the water in one, she quickly heads off upstairs to the bathroom and stands under the shower to freshen up. The heavy head feeling lifts as she washes away the night before and wraps herself in a big fluffy bath towel left out for her by Lou. Shell checks on her friend and sees she is still sound asleep in her bed as she heads back downstairs to get dressed.

Feeling desperate to see Marty again, she puts on her fishnets again from last night with her little denim skirt and white Fred Perry T-shirt, brushes her damp hair and laces up her cherry red boots. She gathers her bags together, closes the door quietly and hurries off to the car. Sitting ready at the wheel, Shell takes a long deep breath and drives into town towards Marty's flat with so many thoughts running through her mind.

She puts on her music to calm he drive. 'It's a Wonderful Life' By The Dualers plays quietly for her and it makes her smile.

Passing Sam's old house, she remembers calling for her mate ready for school and linking arms together, sharing a bag of sherbet pips and sneaking off for a smoke in the lanes with their pack of ten John Player Special and some spearmint gum to follow.

Those days seem like a lifetime away now and Shell wonders how they all got so old, so fast. She pulls up at a housing estate that she had never seen before. The properties all lived in now and a new generation growing up in her old town. She recalls it as being the building site that was there for them to hang out in when they were kids and the huge pipes that they used daily to hide away in or just sit on and listen to music. Daz would've been there with his endless supply of goodies. Sam and Tomo sneaking a kiss at the back and Giff driving her nuts but dancing together to her music on her beloved tape recorder.

Shell wonders how she can remember it all so vividly and yet she can barely remember why she walked into another room at home. It makes her chuckle to herself and drives on with her increasing need to see Marty again.

Passing the old school gates, she glances over and notes the huge fences put up around it now. Life has changed so much since their school days. She recalls running through the gate at top speed with Lou and Sam trying to get away from double maths where they would likely get a ruler across their knuckles from Mr Baker just for being there and breathing too much! And then getting past the window of the deadly Deeson, the miserable head that they all detested so much. Feeling deep love for her mates, she feels a few tears welling up in her eyes. Her vision becomes a little blurred from it and has to stop the car for a moment. She sits still in her seat and dries her eyes. Taking some deep breaths, she pulls herself together and looks across at the sea rolling the waves in, still as it was when she left all those years ago.

Feeling ready to continue, she drives on and pulls up outside the block of flats where Marty lives. She checks her watch and sees it's still only 8.30am but her heart is beating very fast and she gets out of the car to press on the intercom.

It takes a second press for him to answer.

"Yeah? Who is it?" He says, sleepily.

"It's me, Shell. Can I come in?"

He releases the door for her immediately and she eagerly heads off up the stairs to greet him.

"What are you doing here so early woman?" He asks, rubbing his eyes and feeling a little hungover himself. Marty stands there in just his boxer shorts and a UB40 tour T-shirt wondering what is happening.

Dropping her bag on the floor, she wraps her arms around him tightly and kisses him heavily on the lips. Feeling comforted by his tight hug, she finds herself melting into his arms again just like she always did. He takes her through to his bedroom and they sit on the end of the bed together.

"Did you feel just like I did last night on our dare?" Shell asks, stroking his cheek and feeling deep love for him.

"I've always felt it Shell. Come here." He replies, kissing her softly and smiling at the two of them being together. "We seem to have this connection that draws us back together." He quietly plays 'Johnny Too Bad' by UB40 next to the bed and softly kisses her again, knowing what happens next.

She looks into those familiar brown eyes and feels that bond kicking in once again. Untying the laces of her Doc Martens, she giggles a little.

"Only problem with these bloody boots is, they take a while to remove when you're in a hurry. Especially when you have a gorgeous man waiting!"

Marty smiles as he takes off his T-shirt and lays bare waiting for his girl.

Shell stands completely naked with her clothes discarded on the floor and smiles at the sight of him on the bed. Feeling so much love and needing to be close to him, she wastes no time and climbs onto the bed and sits astride of her beautiful man, kissing him slowly and the two of them wrapping themselves together.

*****

"Me and you are so good together ya know." Says Shell, as she lays beside Marty, quietly smoking a cigarette after being loved up in his arms again. "But then I start to remember where I am and wonder how this will all pan out."

"Can't live with me and can't live without me, hey?" Replies Marty, looking a little annoyed and confused at the situation. "You can't keep turning up, doing this and thinking it's going to be ok for fuck's sake."

"I'm so sorry, I think maybe I shouldn't have come and made you think I was back for good." She says, leaning across to kiss his cheek.

"Come back here and live with me girl." He exclaims. "You know I love you to bits and you're right, we would be so good together. I can't think of anything better for the rest of my days. Let's do it hey. I know we'll be so happy together."

"I do love you with all my heart darlin' but I have to go back." She replies with a look of sadness. "This isn't my home and it's too difficult for me here."

Marty rolls his eyes a little and stares out of the window deep in thought.

Shell goes off to the bathroom and throws water on her face abruptly. Standing and staring into the mirror, she closes her eyes for a moment and tries to imagine the scenario of living there with Marty but the memories of her painful past just keep holding her back and she knows it will never happen.

Marty sits on the edge of his bed knowing she is about to go and leave him yet again. He holds his head in his hands and waits.

"I'd better go now." She says, putting her stockings back on and lacing her boots.

"What about me?" He asks, with some anger and sadness in his voice. "How can you just turn up like that and disappear just as fast?"

"I don't wanna leave you boy but I am going to coz I don't want another argument Marty. I don't know what I was thinking coming here and doing this to you. I'm so sorry I'm such a fucked up mess."

She grabs his head and kisses him tightly. With no more to say, she picks up her things and leaves.

"Wow!" He says to himself, as he hears the front door close behind her. "What the fuck was all that about!"

'Dream a Lie' by his beloved favourite band UB40 plays for him as he lays back on to his bed with his head in his hands wondering what she really wants from him.

*****

Shell leaves her car parked in the street below and slowly walks down to the seafront. The day is just warming up and the fresh air helps to clear her mind a little.

She heads on down to the little cove where they all used to run to from school. Climbing over the cliffs and across the rocks to sit and rest, she feels so bad and ashamed about what she just did to her lovely Marty.

She thinks about how the place is still the same after so many years. The seafront seems to have stood still over the years and never moved an inch. She picks up some old dried out seaweed and starts to pop it, just like they used to do as kids. Remembering how they all used to run about dancing across the sand, Shell finds it all too much to take in all alone here so stands up ready to leave but as she does, a whistle is heard from behind.

"Bloody hell! What are you doing here all on your own?" Says Giff, smiling down at her and with Tomo by his side. "Come on Tom, let's get down there mate."

He puts his arm around Shell and kisses her softly on the cheek. Tomo does the same and hugs her tightly.

"Well, I could ask you two the same question." She says, giggling at the sight of their arrival.

"Great minds think alike!" Says Giff, pulling out some cans of beer from his backpack. "Thought we'd have a nose at the old place today after all the great memories last night and of course we can do a bit of hair of the dog I guess!"

"A couple of beers in the sunshine and a few laughs." Adds Tomo, also removing a few more cans of beer from his own bag.

Shell looks at her watch. It's coming up to twelve o'clock and she happily takes a can and sits with the boys, feeling more content now with friends around to comfort her.

"All that's missing here is your bloody tape recorder girl." Laughs Giff. "The beach isn't the same without it."

Shell and Tomo both laugh a little at the thought of her beloved music.

"I can hear it now." She recalls. "All taped every Sunday from the top forty without fail."

"Best times darlin'." Says Giff, with a loving smile.

She begins to tell them about her morning with Marty and how she was drawn to go to his flat after thinking about him all night.

"I love that man with all my heart and soul but we live miles apart and long distance relationships are generally pretty doomed."

"Well, at least you got your leg over, that's the main thing!" He laughs, trying to make everything sound ok and feeling a little at fault for making them kiss and smooch the night before.

Tomo laughs and takes a big swig on his beer, taking in the warmth of the sunshine to his face.

"I haven't been down here for years. Weird how you can live somewhere but forget to visit the places you love." He adds.

Shell starts to feel a little tipsy on the beer after not eating during the morning and the sun beams down on to her head. She gives most of the can back to the boys and pulls out her bottle of water.

"Best not to drink anymore of that, ya know. I'm heading back to London soon." She says, neatening her hair and pulling out a smoke as she takes in the scenery.

"Do you remember all of us over at the old war department just over there?" She points across at the grassy hills and derelict buildings in the distance.

"Bloody hell yeah." Says Tomo, starting to recall the memory. "You're like an old video cassette Shell with it all taped and ready to play inside you girl. Always able to remember stuff we did. I dunno where it all comes from!"

"Well, I do remember it all very clearly. We had some great times down there and so many laughs." She says, taking another gulp of water from the bottle. "One day after school particularly sticks in my head. We were such little shits really, hey! The things we did were stupid and mad."

Shell begins to recall the memory from way back in 1980. "It was a Friday lunch time I remember and we were all ready to skip school and meet over the war department instead of doing double English and Physics."

*****

1980

As Shell sits with her two best mates, Lou and Sam in their Human Biology class, she yawns widely and looks at the big white clock on the wall with complete boredom. The hours and minutes seem never ending and Sam sends a little note along the row to Shell to pass the time, giggling with her mates.

She unravels the little crumpled piece of paper to take a look and in black felt tipped pen it reads….

'**Timmy Rose is having his dick measured with a ruler on the back row!**'

Shell splutters with laughter and is just about to hand it to Lou when the Teacher, Miss Jones, catches sight of it being passed around.

"Shell Rogers!" She bellows across the room. "If you have something interesting going on then please share with the rest of the class right now."

Shell sits still, giggling under her breath.

"Stand up young lady and read aloud what is so extremely hilarious. I'm sure we could all do with brightening our day."

Shell stands at her desk and holds open the note. Sam and Lou put their heads in their hands and wait.

"Timmy Rose is having his dick measured with a ruler on the back row, Miss!" She says loudly, trying not to laugh.

The whole class erupts into a mass of laughter and Timmy Rose turns a bright pink colour with everyone staring at him. Miss Jones is not in the least bit amused and rips the note from Shell's hand. Enraged, she throws it with total disgust into the waste paper bin in the corner of the room, her lips tightly pursed with anger.

"How extremely childish you really are! Get into the corner of the room young lady and stay standing there until home time." She continues to bellow with her face reddening more with every word spoken.

Shell rolls her eyes, huffing and puffing as she strolls over to the wall and slams herself against the side of the blackboard on the way.

As she looks outside, Giff appears and starts snogging the glass of the grubby old window. Shell and the other girls begin to giggle again as Tomo appears beside him, twanging his pair of braces and showing off his new skinhead haircut, parading up and down like a peacock showing off his colourful feathers.

Giff holds a sheet of A4 size paper up to the window with a note written on it in large black lettering.

It reads...

'**SHELL ROGERS GIVES GOOD HEAD ON FRIDAYS'**, with a big smiley face drawn on the side and with a long tongue hanging out. There's a big love heart drawn next to it in red. The whole class erupts with laughter once again and Miss Jones looks like she is about to explode.

She sashays her floaty gypsy skirt across to the window, her hexagonal glasses becoming steamed with anger. Flicking back her mullet of curly black hair, she roars at the boys outside.

"Get away from this window immediately you imbeciles!" Giff and Tomo, amused by it all, begin an erotic dance, thrusting their bodies around and licking their lips seductively at her as she becomes furious and a deep purple colour with embarrassment.

"I know both your names and your form class and you will both be in detention I can promise you that." She barks loudly at them.

"You'll have to catch me first Jonesy!" Says Giff, in a rather silly childish voice. "Come on Tomo let's get out of here."

Tomo pulls out a little silver square packet from his trouser pocket and tears it open to reveal a condom. He quickly blows it up and it becomes a huge balloon. Both begin to laugh uncontrollably as it pops loudly in his own face.

"Suck on that, hippie chick." Says Giff, raising his middle finger and running down the path closely followed by Tomo at his side. Giff then pulls out a small catapult from his pocket and pings a small stone back at the window, laughing madly.

They run across the playground and disappear from view. Sprinting across the car park they see Miss Jone's red Citroen 2CV and Giff empties his sherbet fountain all over her windscreen leaving white powder everywhere.

The boys laugh together mischievously and run towards the lanes before anyone can catch them.

The school bell rings for lunch and the girls jump up, relieved to be free from the boredom of the lesson on human bones.

"Oh man, Giff is such a dick sometimes." Says Shell, giggling with her mates. "He'll be in big shit now!"

"Come on you two, Mr Whippy's in the playground. We'll get an ice cream and get out of here for the afternoon. I'm not staying a minute longer than I have to! Fuck English!" Says Lou, shuffling her mates out of the door.

Linking arms, the girls head over to the bright pink van and think about what sweet treat to have.

"I'm getting a Haunted House." Says Shell, pointing to the huge variety in the picture. "It's my absolute fave."

"Darlek Death Ray for me!" Says Sam, licking her lips and pretending to be a darlek. "EXTERMINATE, EXTERMINATE."

"Oh gotta be a Screwball for me!" Adds Lou, smiling. "Will have my bubblegum ball for later."

Shell opens the purple wrapper and licks the skeleton on her white lolly.

"Come on girls, let's get out of here. I've had enough of this place." She says, leaving the front gates.

Giff and Tomo are waiting patiently and mischievously in the lanes and leap out on them as they approach the bushes, making them jump out of their skin.

"Ah you fuckhead!" Shouts Shell, almost dropping her lolly. "You'd be a dead man if I'd dropped that. You're a lucky fucker!"

"Give us a suck on yours then Shell?" Says Giff, grabbing her hand and sticking his face over the white icey skeleton. "And your lolly!"

Tomo laughs and Sam offers him a bite of her Darlek Death Ray.

"Here comes trouble." Shouts Giff, as Daz pulls up on his bike.

"Alright arseholes! Are we off to the War Dep as planned?" he asks, jumping off his bike.

"Yeah let's go man." Says Giff, lighting up a cigarette and inhaling deeply. "Ready for a few laughs then people. You lot just wait and see what I've got to keep you amused."

*****

The old war department has been a great hideaway for kids to get up to all sorts of mischief and today is no different. Full of derelict buildings and long dark pathways, Shell and her mates love to come here and hang out together, scaring each other and anyone else who passes through.

Wandering into one of their favourite abandoned ruins, the gang sit together on the cold hard ground and Shell takes out her beloved tape recorder.

"Gotta have some decent sounds down here." She says, echoing underground.

Lou takes out a small candle that she took from her mum's drawer at home and lights it with her matches to make a dimly lit den. She drips some of the melted wax on to a box of matches and fixes the candle to it.

"Mum keeps these in case of another power cut." She chuckles.

Shell turns over the cassette and puts it back into the player.

"I'm sure I can hear music outside somewhere ya know." She says, curiously. "I'll drown it out with my own top sounds!" She presses the play button and 'Amigo' By Black Slate comes on.

"Top tune." Says Giff, grinning and opening his bag. "Here ya go, get your lips around this lot."

He takes out two rather large bottles of Woodpecker cider and passes them around.

Sam takes out twenty John Player Special and all take a smoke to have with their drinks.

"This is the life!" Says Lou, looking a little flushed already from her couple of big glugs of alcohol and tapping her feet to the music.

The tape doesn't take a break and goes straight into the next track. 'Ne Ne Na Na Na Na Nu Nu' By Bad Manners and the drinking continues with much singing and giggling.

"I think it's time we had some fun." Says Tomo, mischievously.

He pulls out a little white packet from his Harrington pocket and opens it up. Taking out his maths book, he empties white powder on to the woodchip paper cover and chops it a little with his penknife.

"Here ya go dickheads, have a little snort of whiz and we'll be sorted." He jokes, taking the first line up his nose with a rolled up pound note.

One by one they sniff the powder and immediately start to chatter more, happily drinking and smoking together and getting a wild rush to their heads.

Suddenly the tape cassette slows down and comes to a stop. Shell looks horrified and lifts it out of the player. The brown tape from inside all twisted and knotted stops them in their tracks and the music is no more.

"What the fuck!" Says Shell, distraught at the sight of it all. "That's my best tape that one. All top tunes from last week's top forty. Fuckin' pile of shit!"

She discards the whole tape recorder to the side, devastated at the loss of her favourite sounds and throws the little knotted cassette at the wall with rage.

"What the fuck is that noise out there?" Asks Lou. "I could hear it when we arrived."

"Let's go and check it out then." Says Daz, curiously.

They all get themselves up off the floor and wobble slightly from the effects of the cider. It makes the girls giggle together and they all head outside to listen.

"It's coming from that one over there." Says Sam, pointing towards a little old shelter across the hill.

"Come on, let's go and scare the shit out of them." Says Giff, chuckling through his gulp of cider.

Quietly they wander over the hill and hear the sound of recorders playing.

"Fuckin' hell, who's playing shitty recorders?" Says Daz, trying not to laugh at the bum notes. "Worst musical instrument in the world I reckon!"

"I've got something to scare the shit out of them." Says Giff, reaching into his bag.

"Bound to be a couple of toffs practising for an exam." Laughs Tomo.

Giff pulls out a small cardboard box with colourful cartoon pictures on it.

"What the fuck is that, man?" Asks Daz.

"Indoor fireworks." He replies, grinning widely.

They all laugh as quietly as they can manage, sniggering like Dastardly and Mutley and the girls are all crying as they try to hold in their belly laughs.

Giff takes out a couple of the little fireworks and a box of matches.

"Green smoky grass snake." He reads off one of them. Then "The mini banging bomb." From the other.

It makes them all laugh even more.

"What the fuck are they all about?" Asks Shell, quietly chuckling to herself.

Giff places them at the entrance and lights the wick on both.

"You'll see. Move now, come on you lot quick as ya can." He says, beckoning them all to hide behind a bush nearby.

'THUD' 'POP' 'BANG' 'FIZZ' the noises begin and smoke starts to bellow into the pathway. The recorders stop and the girls screaming begins.

'THUD' 'POP' 'BANG' 'FIZZ' goes again and a green slimy looking snake unravels from the box making them all laugh even more.

"Fuck, they are bigger than I thought!" Laughs Giff, falling over slightly sozzled.

As the noises stop, two girls emerge in tears with blackened faces and ruined school uniform.

"It's Clare Hawkes and Alice Church." Whispers Lou.

"Ah the two boffins of the year!" Laughs Shell.

They all fall into a heap giggling as they watch the two girls walk off in floods of tears dragging their recorders and blackened music books along behind them.

Just then, Carnage appears from nowhere.

"Thought I'd find you tossers here." He says, wandering up to them and looking as mischievous as always.

"Bothering young girls again, hey Giff?" He laughs, winking at them. "I've got something even better. Give us a swig on that cider and I'll make it a day to remember for ya."

Giff gives him the bottle and waits to see what he has to offer.

All of them are quite tipsy by now and can't stop giggling. Carnage gulps down the cider and wipes his mouth dry handing it back to Giff.

"Right then." Announces Carnage, pointing to another area of the war department. "Over at the back there is mod Ron and his bird. They are havin' it off behind the gate." He continues, reaching into his parka and pulling out two fireworks.

The gang all laugh at the thought of what's going on over there and look intrigued as to what Carnage has planned.

"Shit! They're fuckin' bangers." Laughs Daz.

"Watch and learn children, watch and learn." Adds Carnage, wandering over to the gate in his usual destructive way.

The others hide behind a bush and wait for the show to begin.

Lighting the two fireworks, he throws them quickly inside one of the old war ruins and runs to hide.

'BOOM' 'BOOM'

The noise is extremely loud, echoing inside the derelict building. It makes some of the rubble fall from the walls and ceiling and sends smoke and dust bellowing out of the entrance.

Ron and his girl quickly jump out covered in black dust looking completely shocked and stunned. The two of them cough and splutter from the smoke and dust.

"Who the fuck did that?" He shouts, angrily with just his ruined Secret Affair T-shirt on and his genitalia blackened along with the rest of his body.

His girl leaps out of the hole in just her skimpy black knickers. She tries to cover her tiny breasts, all black and dusty and begins to cry.

"I know it's you Carnage, you fucked up shitbag. I'm gonna punch your lights out wanker! If you've as much as touched my parka I'll fuckin' kill you man!"

He catches sight of an unruly Carnage and gives chase. His darkened and dusty body parts bouncing along as he picks up speed and grabs him from behind, smacking him straight on the nose and knocking him firmly to the ground.

Leaving him flat out, he strolls back triumphantly to his girl huddled in a corner.

"Fuckin' arsehole deserved that!" He says, proudly. "If my Lambretta is damaged he will seriously regret ever knowing me, I swear!"

"Time for a quick exit me thinks." Says Daz, quietly to the others behind the bush.

"Yep I'm outta here. That was enough for me." Says Shell, becoming increasingly paranoid from their earlier sniffing and alcohol.

They look over at Carnage, completely spark out on the grass.

"He'll be up again in a bit." Laughs Giff. "Come on we're done here."

They all run quickly towards the exit, laughing at their afternoon of chaos.

"Better than double Physics." Says Tomo, giggling.

"Yeah, Carnage is always an accident waitin' to happen." Laughs Lou.

"More cider anyone?" Says Giff, with a cheeky smile.

*****

"Blimey this place sure is so full of memories hey!" Says Tomo, with a smile.

"Sure is mate. We never knew we were making memories. We thought we were just havin' a good laugh." Replies Giff, finishing his can of beer. "I think Carnage had a broken nose and two black eyes from big Ron if I remember rightly."

"Yeah he did. He stayed away from everyone for a few weeks it was really quiet without him." Replies Tomo, laughing at the memory.

"Well, it was the best time of my life for sure." Continues Tomo, looking around at the beach and the cliffs.

"You lot are so lucky." Says Shell, looking deeply at the boys. "You never had anything to make you sad here. I had so many shitty memories to deal with and I still do. And I'm screwing up Marty's life along with mine!"

"You need to sort out what you want in life mate. Can't keep messin' with his feelings girl. He's a top bloke and doesn't deserve it." Says Giff.

"I gotta go home now and sort myself out." She replies. "We're out at our Specials night very soon so I'm gonna go away and think hard about what I'm doing. Gotta see Dan and Alex and maybe my friends Ruth and Jo. Get my head together and stop hurting myself and others."

"Love ya both so much and thanks for the night at Lou's it was amazing as always with you lot."

Shell hugs her mates and gets herself together to head back to London.

"See ya in a week or so darlin', it's gonna be a top night for us all so get your head sorted girl. Put all the heavy stuff behind you and move on, hey?" Says Giff, kissing her cheek.

"Yeah love ya too." Says Tomo. "Keep strong and sort your shit out."

"See ya next week then lads. New me, no more tears." She replies, giving them a wave and blowing a kiss as she heads off back to the car.

Shell wanders along the street towards her car feeling pretty down about herself and where she has ended up in her life. She sits in the driver's seat of her little Fiat 500 and puts her head on the steering wheel as she thinks about heading back to London to see her beautiful boy, Alex.

She looks up at the flats again where Marty lives and sighs heavily.

With her mind full of doubts, she starts her engine and begins the long drive back to London. Clicking on to her music in the car, 'Inner London Violence' By Bad Manners comes on and she smiles to herself thinking it's a very apt song for the journey as she heads off up the motorway towards the city.

Chapter 6

Strolling slowly across Westminster Bridge, Shell breathes in the dusty city air and smells the fumes of the iconic red buses and black cabs taking so many people on their journeys around London.

The River Thames below is glistening in the evening sunshine and everyone is in such a hurry around her. She takes in the sight of the beautiful Big Ben and the Houses of Parliament, admiring their presence.

Much of her life starts to fall into place in her mind. She had run away all those years ago and tried to become someone new. Someone with no difficult past to contend with and mostly it had worked for her.

Her and Dan had loved and cared deeply for each other. Both running away from separate places and different scenarios but held together by their need to be someone and somewhere else. The anonymity of the city making it a perfect retreat for them for so many years.

Leaning over the bridge and staring at the sight of the huge London Eye, Shell feels a heavy weight in her heart and soul.

The man she had loved for all of her time in London, now estranged from her and their bond broken.

And then the man she left behind all those years ago in the sadness of that little town, coming back into her life after so long, still with so much love for her after all she put him through.

Wandering a little further, Shell enters a small bar that she and her friends had used on many occasions and orders a beer. 'Connected' by Stereo MCs blasts from the speaker in the corner and it immediately reminds her of a time in the nineties with her beloved Dan and best friends Ruth and Jo. She sits alone in the window staring at the passers-by and feels the alcohol start to numb the hurt of all those years gone by.

She takes another and another and begins to feel some of the heartache ease a little. Needing a shoulder to cry on, she takes out her phone from her bag and decides to call her friend of many years, Ruth.

Feeling rather tipsy and with no food inside her, she makes her phone call.

"Hey Shell, so good to hear from you. You ok darling? Been meaning to call for a beer but you know how it is." Answers Ruth.

"No I'm really not ok." Shell Replies, slightly slurring and becoming a little tearful. "I've fucked up my whole life and I need you mate."

"Where are you sweetheart?" Asks Ruth, feeling worried for her dear friend.

Shell tells her exactly where she is and Ruth says to wait there and she's on her way.

Shell takes yet another beer and drowns her sorrows, becoming more and more drunk and alone.

*****

Ruth arrives to find Shell slumped on the table in the corner by the window, looking forlorn and full of sorrow.

"Oh my darling, what are you doing all alone like this?" Ruth asks, lifting her friend's head from the table. "Oh man, you look like shite girl! What are we gonna do with you? This is not like you at all. You're a happy girl who loves life."

"Sorry mate." She mutters, wobbling her head and feeling quite ashamed.

"Come on, we're going off to the coffee shop up the road to try and sober you up a bit." Says Ruth, lifting her by the arm and carrying her slightly out of the door.

A few smug couples snigger at the state of her as she attempts to act normal when leaving and some small groups of young lads giggle together about her as the old drunk woman in the corner.

Ruth looks at them all with evil eyes as she leaves and makes it known that she's not amused by their behaviour.

Struggling with her friend down the street, Ruth manages to sit her at a small round table outside the shop, thinking the fresh air will be best for her.

She orders some coffees and takes them back outside to her tearful friend.

"Oh Ruth, it's all finished. I'm done with. Unloved and unwanted." She says, woefully. "What the fuck have I done?"

"I know I ran away to block it all out. I didn't expect to find true love in Dan but I did and we became a brand new set of people." She continues. "I never had to remember any of the past after that, but now look at me. I have no one and nothing and don't even know what I want or where I belong anymore."

Shell begins to sob desperately at her state of affairs. Her black eye liner now smudging all over her eyes and cheeks like an Alice Cooper lookalike at the end of a sweaty gig. Ruth sits holding her hand and listening like a good friend always does.

"My life broke me back then ya know. I couldn't stand to be in that town a moment longer with all that shit baggage to handle."

"I wanted my mum so badly and nothing I could ever do would bring her back to me."

"I watched my dad destroy himself on the whisky, his skin and eyes becoming more and more yellow every day as he slowly rotted his liver and finished himself off with no thought for me."

Shell takes a breath and sighs heavily before continuing.

"I look back and think how could all this happen to such an innocent young girl? It's just too hard for you to understand the pain and depression I had growing up. I hate putting all this shit on you mate but I'm really struggling."

Ruth strokes her friend's arm and comforts her as best she can.

"I'm here for you darling." She says.

"Oh Ruth, I've loved being back in contact with my dearest old friends but I've had to relive it all in that town with so many tears and gut-wrenching memories. Maybe it just wasn't the right thing to do after all."

Shell Sighs heavily again and wipes away a few blackened tears with her sleeve, staining her green scrap jacket with dripping make-up.

"Oh darling, hindsight is a wonderful thing. I'm so sorry that you had such a shit time. None of us really knew quite how bad it had been as you kept it all inside." Says Ruth, taking both of her hands tightly.

"You're stronger than this girl. Come on, I've got a little something to help your head." She says, a little mischievously. "Obviously coffee is not the way forward! Come on, come to the loo with me right now."

Following her dear friend through the café and to the toilets, they head into a cubicle together like a couple of naughty teenagers. It makes Shell giggle for the first time that evening.

"Here, have a little snifter on that." Says Ruth, opening a little paper wrap. "Always got a little something for emergency use, even at my age!"

She winks at Shell and they both chuckle a little.

"Never too old for a little of what you fancy. Come and play with Charlie!" Continues Ruth, offering her a half size straw. Shell puts it into her nostril and sniffs hard on the long line of white powder.

"Oh man, I've not done this stuff for a while mate." Says Shell, rinsing her face with cold water and pulling herself together. "Woah! Straight to my head, I'm buzzin' girl."

"See, you really can still laugh and be that strong girl I used to know." Says Ruth, sniffing through the straw herself.

"Oh yeah, I feel pretty good now." She adds, re-applying her lipstick and eye liner in the mirror.

"That's it my girl, let's get out of here and go party on for a bit, hey!" Says Ruth, feeling a huge buzz herself and trying not to keep sniffing too much as they prepare themselves to leave.

The girls straighten themselves up, check their look in the mirror and head off out of the café toilets and start to walk through the city.

"I just love buzzin' through all the nightlife here Ruth. Best place in the world for me." Says Shell, striding fast and taking in everything around her.

"And me too mate. I can't imagine being anywhere else in the world." Replies Ruth. "Let's sit on the bench by the park over there for a bit. It's a lovely evening and the fresh air will give us a good head rush."

"Stay there Shell. I'll run over and grab a couple of cans for us." She adds, placing her friend on the old wooden bench and hurriedly crossing the road to the local off licence.

Sitting quietly alone, Shell takes in her surroundings and feels love for her city. She feels at home again thinking of the fantastic years she's had here and all that she has done with Dan and Alex and all her lovely friends that she made over her life in London.

Ruth arrives back a little out of breath and smiles as she hands her a can of pina colada.

"There ya go darlin', cocktails at the bench to watch the city life go by." Says Ruth, giggling with her dear friend.

"Oh just what I need. That gear is hot stuff Ruth. I've not buzzed like that for a while." Shell laughs and holds her friend's hand. "Thanks for picking me up mate. I've had a few difficult days and probably need to reset my world. I'd forgotten what it was like to have a few drinks and a head rush. It's definitely making me smile again."

"Hey, that's what friends are for, ya know. I don't give a shit that you're slurring and falling over a table. I'll always be there to pick you up and clean up your mess just as you would for me."

They both giggle a little with the effects of the drugs and alcohol.

"Hey, I love it here. Just a little drink and couple of lines with my good friend. What more could I ask for in life?" Says Shell, feeling thankful for her mate picking her up when she was so down.

"Ya know, sitting here with you on this bench reminds me of back in the nineties. Me, you and Jo out on the razzle ending up at that nightclub, Lonelys and those fellas we met totally weird and smashed. Wow, do you remember?" Asks Shell, feeling reminiscent.

"I most certainly do Shell. The picture of them is ingrained on to my brain!" She laughs. "Just one line of this shit and we are always hook, line and sinker!"

"We had the best time just dancing all night without a care in the world but we always talk too much crap on that stuff and attract dodgy men!" Shell laughs.

"That club was so dark and had little corners where you could disappear with a partner or your mates and be out of sight, getting up to all sorts. Continues Shell. "It had a disco ball on the ceiling I remember and the music was amazing for dancing all night."

"We were always dressed to kill and danced off our faces with anyone who wanted to join us." Laughs Ruth.

"At the end of that night, those three guys were done in on E tabs." Shell recalls. "We came out of the club smashed and there they were, all completely naked and hammered and asking us to take them home to their mums! They were crying and paranoid, I think they just did far too much that night."

Both girls laugh loudly at the memory of arranging a cab for the three fellas to get home and who had no idea where any of their clothes were.

"It took me seven different cab drivers to find one that would accept the naked men and get them home." Shell giggles. "No idea what ever happened to them or if they actually got home that night after I bundled them into the back of a black cab."

"We've had some great nights out in London Shell." Says Ruth, putting her arm around her friend. "I wouldn't change a thing. All the amazing gigs we've been to together and the raves and festivals. We couldn't have had a better time really."

"Me neither, I wouldn't change it for the world. I've had a great time here. It's always felt like home to me."

An old but totally restored blue Ford Escort Mark 2 pulls up at the traffic lights in front of them and 'Money' by The Flying Lizards is pumping out of the sound system inside. The ageing fella inside looks over and winks at the girls making them smile and the two of them sing along to the lyrics.

"Wow, just look at that Ruth. It's the same as Marty had all those years ago. His beloved car was his life." Says Shell, with a huge grin.

The lights change to green and the car speeds off leaving the girls with a beautiful memory.

"Ah what a fantastic car, mate." Replies Ruth, hugging her friend. "I bet that left you with goose bumps seeing an identical car like that."

Shell sighs and takes a huge swig from her can.

"Wow that was some memory passing me in the street. Do you think it's trying to tell me something Ruth?" Asks Shell.

"Maybe so darlin'. Maybe so."

"How's your lovely boy these days Shell? Is he still doing gigs with Dan?" Asks Ruth. "What a gorgeous boy you brought up. He's an absolute credit to you and Dan."

"He's doing great thanks. He's just my world. I love him to bits. He's playing in Camden with Dan right now, they have a new covers band apparently and both loving it he tells me. I've not seen them but I'm sure they are amazing as always."

"Oh come on Shell, let's get a cab and go watch them. It'll be great to see them again. What do you say darlin'?" Asks Ruth, eager to go and watch some live music.

"Why not." Says Shell. "Go and hail a cab then girl and we'll go check it out."

Ruth stands at the side of the road and watches for a cab with a yellow lit hire sign. She looks excited and smiles over at Shell rubbing her hands together.

She holds out her arm to show that she needs one to stop and a lovely black electric cab pulls up beside her.

"Camden please, Dublin Castle." She says, hopping into the back with Shell.

"This will be fun." Says Ruth, huddling up to her mate in the cab. "I haven't seen them for ages and love their music. Both of them are so talented."

"I haven't seen Dan for a good while either Ruth so I hope it's not going to be awkward."

The cab trundles off into the evening traffic and the girls watch out of the window at the sights going by.

"I just love being in a London cab and watching the city go by." Says Ruth, gazing at the crowds going about their business.

"Yeah, best way to travel in style!" Laughs Shell.

"You been busy?" She shouts to the driver.

"Up and down girl. Will be getting a bit busier now as everyone's on their way out for the night." Replies the cabbie. "Have a great evening both of ya."

The cab pulls up in Camden and the girls jump out in front of the venue and pay the driver, thanking him for the journey with a few pounds tip.

Ruth takes hold of her friend's arm and looks excited to be there but Shell looks nervous and hesitant as they walk together.

"You ok darlin'?" Asks Ruth kindly, as they wander up towards the door. "I'm sure it will be just fine and Dan will be happy to see us."

"Ok, let's go and do it." She replies, apprehensively. "What could possibly go wrong?"

Entering the bar area, the room smells a little stale of big nights gone by.

"It smells so old in here." Laughs Shell, "Fantastic little venue though. One of my favourites. I've been here so many times now."

Ruth giggles and squeezes through the crowds of drinkers at the bar to get served.

"Smells of pubs and Wormwood Scrubs!" She laughs. "Love those words."

'Green Onions' by Booker T. & the M.G.'s is playing loudly and makes Shell smile at the great music.

Finally getting a couple of beers, the girls find a little corner to chat. The venue is busy and the noise of groups of friends chatting and drinking makes them raise their voices to hear each other.

"Wasn't expecting it to be so crowded." Says Shell, loudly.

"Nah, me neither but it's good for the band to have such a great turnout." Ruth replies, staying close to her mate.

"Can't see anyone I know so far." Says Shell, taking a sip on her beer. "They will be the first band on so we could go through to the stage if you like."

Ruth agrees and the two of them slip through the crowd and up to the main door.

"Evening ladies." Says the beefy bouncer on the door. "Tickets on the door are a tenner each. You havin' a good night so far?"

Ruth takes out her cash and pays for them both to get in.

"So far so good, cheers." Replies Ruth, eager to get through to the main stage.

"Nice one girls. Enjoy your night." He says, opening the heavy door for them and holding it as they walk through. The room is already pretty full of youngsters looking quite drunk and acting loud and stupid. The girls look at one another and Shell raises her eyebrow with a chuckle.

It starts to hit home that they are getting old and don't really fit in at these gigs anymore. Shell looks at her friend and wonders how they got to being in their fifties so fast.

"I blinked and we were fifty mate! Look at how young they all are." Says Ruth, shaking her head. "How did we become the oldies? It's only when I come out like this I realise how much older than everyone I am!"

The DJ is still on the stage before the band and is banging out some seriously loud music that the girls have never heard of and it makes them feel slightly awkward and ancient.

"Not a clue mate." Shell shrugs at the sounds going on in the room.

They both laugh together as they try to work out if they know any of the music at all.

Suddenly Shell catches sight of Dan in the corner of the room. Her heart sinks a little as he has his arm lovingly wrapped around another woman and is laughing and joking with her. She stares at the sight of him for a moment as he kisses that familiar looking girl on the cheek and strokes her hair.

Ruth spots it at the same time and both are silent in the moment.

"I'm not sure this was such a good idea mate." Says Shell, quietly watching and feeling increasingly uncomfortable.

"Oh mate, I hadn't even thought about Dan being in another relationship."

"Fuck! That's Jess Middleton." She announces, as her stomach begins to feel sick. "Oh man why her for fuck's sake?"

Shell quickly makes her way out of the hall and into the ladies toilets. She closes the door on the cubicle and takes a huge deep breath. Nothing could've prepared her to see that. Her stomach hurts and she holds it tightly as a couple of tears fall on to her lap.

"Shell, where are you darlin'?" Shouts Ruth, worriedly. "Come out mate. Don't be alone in there. I'm so sorry it was my idea to come here."

Shell opens the door and throws her arms around her friend. She breaks down in tears, sobbing on to Ruth's shoulder.

"Now I know what it did to Dan when I met up with Marty again." She cries. "What a real shit I am. I need to get out of here Ruth. I'm sorry but this was such a bad idea coming here. I could've taken anything but that Jess Middleton. Why her?"

"Ok darlin', let's get you out of here. It wasn't one of our better moves." Agrees Ruth, shuffling her to the door.

As they make their way swiftly into the venue again, Dan is stood there right in front of them with the woman that they both remember well. He looks straight across at the two of them and his face seems to drop at the sight.

Jess Middleton turns and looks her straight in the eyes and her gaze says it all. That look from a female in complete triumph is thrown with a vengeance at Shell and she knows she has lost this time.

Shell keeps her head high and manages to hold it together as they pass. Both girls scurry out of the door and on to the street wondering why they chose to come in the first place.

"Oh hell, I'm so sorry I don't want to leave you alone here but I need the loo badly Shell. Just stay out here and I'll be as quick as I can, ok."

Shell nods and props herself up against the wall to wait.

She lifts one of her cherry red boots high in the air and thinks about Dan and the best times they had together. She wonders if Jess Middleton was making him happy or if she just wanted to get back at her for the fight they had. She wipes her eyes with an old tissue from her jacket pocket and stuffs it back up her sleeve.

Dan walks out of the bar and on to the street. He looks around and seeing her standing alone at the side of the pub, he slowly and awkwardly walks up to see her.

"Shell, what are you doing here?" He asks, softly. "That's not the way for you to find out I have someone new in my life. I'm sorry you had to see that."

"Really Dan? Jess Middleton?" That would be the person I would despise most in this world and if you did it to hurt me then you have definitely achieved that so well done!!"

Dan stands quietly letting things settle down a bit. He doesn't say a word, just waits.

After a few moments Shell speaks again.

"Hey, I hope she's everything you dream of Dan. You deserve the best and I'm sorry for being a fucked up twat."

"Shell, you and me have had an amazing time together and we can still be the best of friends if you want to but we aren't together now." He explains, with a hint of sadness in his voice. "You can't have it all you know. I need to have a life as well."

"I'm so sorry for everything. I don't know what I want in this life anymore. I just know I've messed up most of it. Please don't tell Alex I was here. I don't want him to worry that he didn't tell me about you and your new relationship."

Dan kisses her cheek softly and strokes her hair.

"I'll always love you Shell. Oh and for the record, I didn't do it to hurt you. I did it because you left me and I can also have a life like you." He says, touching her arm as he walks away into the venue.

Staring into space, Shell realises that it really is all over and she has nothing left but her beautiful boy and her friendships. She feels her heart ripping apart inside her.

"Hey, you ok darlin'?" Asks Ruth, returning from inside and wrapping her arm around her friend's shoulder.

"Time to go home I think mate. I'm getting too old for all this."

The girls link arms and wander over to the side of the road to hail another cab and head for home.

 "Jess Middleton for fuck's sake." Says Ruth. "Wow. Didn't see that coming. Anyway I'm so glad you punched that smirk off her face that night back then when we first met her!"

"Me too." Replies Shell. "And I'd do it again if she ever passes me in the street!"

Ruth takes hold of her arm and punches it into the air.

"You're the strongest girl I know and you'll get through all this shit. She will never have the years that you had with your lovely Dan, you know Shell."

Shell nods and pulls herself together holding on tightly to her friend.

"Oh man, still can't get a cab. It's taking forever." Says Ruth, frantically waving her arms out to draw attention in their need to get home.

"I need to go back inside and use the loo too Ruth." Says Shell, hesitantly moving off to the pub again. "Sorry I will be as quick as I can."

"Oh wait darlin'. I'm not leaving you to go off alone." Replies Ruth, shuffling her friend back into the door.

"I won't be long." Adds Shell, opening the door to the ladies and leaving her friend by the bar.

Locking the door behind her in one of the cubicles, Shell sits down and wishes she had never come to the gig. She feels the lasting effects of the drug making her feel cold chills and a numbness from the alcohol.

Feeling both anger and sadness, she adjusts her clothing and gets herself together again. Opening the cubicle door, Shell walks across to the hand basin, washes her hands and looks in the mirror. She looks tired and drained from a lack of sleep and a lack of food.

As she stares at her watery eyes, the door opens behind her and in the mirror she sees the smirking face of Jess Middleton strutting behind her.

Feeling the wave of resentment and rage inside her, Shell turns quickly and grabs hold of the girl's hair, pushing her smug face up against the wall from behind.

"Don't ever look at me with that smug fuckin' grin again or I'll wipe it clean off your face. Understand me?" Shell says, shaking with anger and desperate to knock her to the ground.

"Completely." Replies Jess, only just able to get a word out as her face is squashed against the stone wall and her hair held tight behind her head.

"You might be with Dan for now but it won't last as he will quickly suss you out and remember that you will never have what I had with him for all those years so keep your shitty looks to yourself and fuck off."

Shell begrudgingly lets go of her hair and Jess hurries off into a cubicle.

"If I ever hear you've mentioned this conversation to Dan, I'll come looking for you." Says Shell, quietly against the cubicle door.

"Understood." Comes the soft reply from behind the door.

Feeling stronger and slightly more accomplished, Shell heads off out the door and grabs Ruth from the bar area ready to leave.

"Everything ok darlin'? Asks Ruth, as they head over to try for another cab.

"Everything is just fine." Says Shell, feeling quite fulfilled by her trip to the ladies. "Everything is just fine now."

*****

Pulling up at Shell's place, Ruth hugs her tightly and waves her friend off from the cab. Shell walks alone up to her front door feeling drained of all her emotions.

"I'm just at the end of the phone darlin' any time day or night." Shouts Ruth from the cab window. "Love ya mate."

She waves back to acknowledge her dear friend, puts the key into the lock and goes inside, closing the door behind her. She stands still against the back of it wondering how she got so old and tired and how everything went so wrong.

She stares at the wall and sighs heavily. The pictures of Dan and little Alex looking down on her, reminding her of their life together and the silence of the place makes her feel so very lonely.

Throwing off her jacket in a heap on the floor and untying her boots she wanders into the kitchen and pours herself another large glass of wine. She takes a huge mouthful and closes her eyes for a moment.

Wandering back into the lounge she puts on some music and flops down heavily onto the sofa, spilling some of her wine over her Fred Perry T-shirt.

'Step On' By Happy Mondays blares out in the room. It makes her smile at the thoughts of the early nineties with Dan and her best mates in London, Ruth and Jo.

"Sort your fuckin' head out girl!" She says out loud to herself. "You're stronger than all these tears. Get a fuckin' grip on it."

She pulls out her phone and sees a message alert. It's from Lou.

"Hey Shell, hope you're ok darlin'? Don't forget our gig a week Monday for all of us. All sorted and can't wait to do it all again. Love ya, keep skankin'."

"As if I'm gonna forget that!!" She says to herself.

Shell smiles at the thought of their night out. Seeing The Specials probably for the last time with her old friends will surely be something truly amazing.

The picture of Dan with Jess Middleton continues to play heavily in her mind and she drinks her wine quickly to ease the pain.

Taking a deep breath, Shell puts down her glass of wine on the side table and falls asleep curled up on the sofa all alone.

Chapter 7

After a few long days of working through her life issues, it's finally time now for all the old friends to have their big night out together and jumping off the tube at Waterloo, Shell feels a rush of excitement for the evening ahead, knowing she is about to watch her musical heroes again for the first time in years and with all her best old skanking mates too. She looks around at the hustle and bustle of the tube platform and feels a wave of love for the city she's called home for so many wonderful years. She has that Friday feeling in her stomach, the one she loves so much only this time it feels stronger and makes her breathe faster.

She takes herself to the main train station and heads nervously towards the clock, recalling that evening four years ago when everything changed and her world turned upside down. When she held up that little white flower as her amazing little group of friends arrived and her heart felt full again.

Standing still for a moment inside the station, she looks around at the mass of people hurrying past and wonders how she got there. To be in her fifties but to still feel like that crazy teenager in her heart.

Looking down at her cherry Doc Martens, she smiles at them and thinks of all they have been through with her. Glancing back up at her watch, she sees it's ten to eight and her hand catches her eye. Looking thin and ageing and with her pretty silver ring from Dan still gleaming on her finger, it makes a lump in her throat and she swallows quickly and wipes away a stray tear with her sleeve. Not really knowing whether it's a happy tear or a sad one, she looks to the ground and stands numb for a moment.

With so many thoughts racing through her mind, she starts to gather herself together and heads towards the beautiful old clock that holds deep memories for her but before she can reach it, a hand grabs her shoulder.

"Marty!" She says, a little shocked as she turns to see who it is.

"Hi ya." He says, with a wink and a smile. "You ok?"

Shell kisses his cheek.

"Thanks darlin'. I can't tell you how happy I am that you came. We're gonna skank to The Specials tonight! How fuckin' cool is that? Me, you and all the others. The night of our lives!"

"Yeah it's gonna be a top night." He replies, happily. "Before we go and meet the others, I just wanna say sorry. I've been a bit of a wanker. It's always about me and I'm always so fuckin' needy. I'm really sorry. Me and Alex are getting on really well and my head is more sorted now I think." He says, with an air of confidence. "I'm still in love with you, ya know but I'm starting to understand the feelings you have for the town and for your home now in London. I'm ready to do friends and whatever else we manage along the way now coz that's what we all are isn't it, a gang of best mates who've been given the chance to enjoy each other again after so many years apart."

"Oh Marty, yeah we are and I love you very much but this is my world and London is my life. We can have great times ahead of us you know."

They take each other in their arms tightly and feel a sense of relief.

"Come on, let's get to that clock and find the others and do what we all do best, skank it up all night!" Says Shell, giggling and staring into his deep brown eyes with love.

He kisses her forehead with a smile.

"What are you waitin' for then woman? Come on, I wanna check out your best skankin' moves! Never too old to get your skankin' boots moving."

Linking arms with him, they head over to the clock excitedly and sit on the bench to wait.

"Do you promise to stay talking to me this time?" Asks Shell. "And make sure you have time with Alex like we first planned?"

"I do. I've been a total arsehole ignoring friends and hiding away and I'm ready to be a good dad to Alex and a top friend with you. And maybe we can see each other sometimes. No more crap from me. I'm done with all that."

"Wow, loving the new Marty! I could fall for a man like you!" She replies with a naughty grin.

"I'm sorry too darlin'." She says, stroking his cheek. "I shouldn't have come over like that so early in the morning and left just like that. It was so very wrong. It won't happen again."

"Come on, let's go find the others, hey? And have the night of our lives."

*****

"I'm feelin' hot tonight Tom." Says Giff, strutting along like a teenager again. "Fuckin' years have fallen off me these last few weeks. I feel like I'm back at West Way again with you lot and ready for anything!"

"I tell ya what mate, I've missed this so much. I don't care how old I am, I'm ready for the night of my life." Replies Tomo, full of energy.

"Me too." Adds Daz, trying to keep up with their pace. "I'm buzzin' big time."

You lads look bloody smart as hell tonight." Says Sam, smiling at the sight of them all.

"Yeah I'm pretty impressed, you might even get a snog tonight." Laughs Lou.

"Oh man, give it to me now." Shouts Giff, with a cheeky grin. "I'm always ready, willing and able."

The gang giggle lovingly together as they head up towards the clock. Five pairs of Doc Martens walking side by side, tightly laced and shiny, they quietly stride along with huge pride.

Each one of them dressed in a black Fred Perry T-shirt with yellow trim, jeans with perfect turn ups and green scrap jackets, smiling at one another, bonded by their passion for music and love for each other.

Giff begins to sing softly as they approach the clock and the others join in, one by one and get louder and louder as they go.

As Marty and Shell sit together having a laugh on the bench, they hear a group of people behind singing a Madness song...

'It Must Be Love, Love, Love.'

"Oh here we go!" Says Shell, rolling her eyes at the gang arriving in full song. "Hey you lot, nice one!"

"Alright babe?" Says Giff, with a sweet smile and a wrap of his arms around her. "Missed ya!"

"Missed you too mate!"

"Come here!" Says Daz, storming through everyone for a hug. "Can't wait for tonight. Gonna be totally brilliant."

The whole group swarm in together with arms around each other as they always did, just like that huge rugby scrum.

"Good to see you here Marty." Says Tomo. "We are complete for a top night!"

"All looking dapper tonight you lot." Says Marty. "Good to see a circle of Doc Martens in front of me. I feel top skankin' coming on!"

"Well I'm ready for a few beers, I don't know about you lot!" Says Lou, giggling.

"Me too, I'm well up for a good night. Got that Friday feelin' Shell?" Asks Sam, jumping up and down like a teenager back in time.

"Oh man, I'm so ready for this. I decided it would be great to go back to the Embankment to remember that night we met under the clock and went off on that 2-Tone cruise up the Thames so I've got a few bottles of beer in my bag and I'm paying for the best London black cabs for all of us and then back later to the gig with no arguments so let's get a move on and head for the taxi rank." Says Shell, taking control of the night.

The gang all start to cheer and move off happily with a spring in their step.

*****

Marty and Shell take the first cab and the others pile into the ones behind, heading off for their special evening.

"Can't believe this is happening and we are all off to see The Specials together in 2019 Marty. Where have the fuckin' years gone." Says Shell, shaking her head in disbelief. "I really wish my life had started out better. Things may have been so different. All the tears that town has given me over the years. I swear I will never let it have a hold on me again. I will never live there again Marty. If you want to see me, you'll have to come to London."

"Fair enough. It's screwed your head up for sure, I can see that." He replies, wrapping a gentle arm around her shoulder in the back seat of the cab. "Don't cry about it anymore. Just think of the good times we all had and the friendships it gave us."

"I will. I'm done with that place. This is my home and the tears for that town are all dried up. Now then, I have to remind you that Dan and Alex are going to be at the gig tonight. I'm hoping you will all manage to be civil to each other."

"I will just for you Shell." Replies Marty. "And for Alex. We have to try anyway."

"Thanks. I know this is hard for you." She says, kissing his cheek. "Come on, we're here."

Unclipping their seatbelts and hopping out of the cab, they pay the driver, thanking him with a large tip.

They wander over to meet the others and all stroll side by side up the Embankment, breathing in the life and love of London and the adrenaline begins pumping in anticipation of the gig making them feel ready to enjoy their memories once again.

Shell pulls out a bottle of beer for each of her friends and smiles at the sight of them all together again.

"Blimey how did we get here to be so old?" Says Daz, sipping on his beer. "One minute you're a teenager havin' a laugh with ya mates then your old and struggling to walk, let alone skank!"

"I love you all ya know." Replies Shell. "The bond we all have is so big and unbreakable. I can't wait to dance with you all tonight."

Giff leaps up skanking and begins to sing at the top of his voice.

"Too Much Too Young!" He shouts, as he twists his ankle and trips up. "Ouch! For fuck's sake!"

They all laugh as he lands flat out on the pavement.

"Well I suppose I've really done a bit too much and now I'm getting too old!" He giggles. "You know, I'm not quite as fast on my toes as I was!"

"Do you all remember when we were here last? We were slaughtered singing 'Do Nothing' by The Specials strutting up the Embankment in our DMs with our beers."

"What a night that was." Replies Lou, smiling at the memory.

"I wanna do it again. Come on, walk with me with pride all the way back up to the cab rank." Says Shell, gathering them all up together.

All seven of them line up ready to walk together. They look lovingly at one another and feel a strong bond of friendship as the memory of their school days rushes into their minds. Shell starts to sing and they all join in with the lyrics that meant the world to them back in 1981.

"I walk and walk, do nothing...." they sing together in unison at the top of their voices as they stride seven pairs of Doc Martens all in line.

It brings a lump to Shell's throat to see them all together singing and makes her smile broadly.

"Loved that so much." She says, as they reach the top. "Can't wait to dance with my besties tonight."

"We'll dance while we've still got legs that work and sing while we've still got teeth to show off!" Giggles Daz.

"Cheers you lovely lot." Says Giff, holding up his beer bottle to them all.

"Cheers!" They all shout together and clank their glass bottles together with a smile.

"Come on you old gits, let's finish our beers and head off to the gig. I for one can't wait for tonight." Says Shell, downing the last of her drink. "Time for our skank up to the best band in the whole of the universe...."

Excitedly Entering the Forum and grabbing their beers from the bar, the gang all get themselves into the stalls in anticipation of what's to come and get ready for all the memories to take them to their special place.

'Red Light' by The Dualers is pumping out in the background as the place warms up and gives them all a smile.

Marty heads off to the loo, leaving his pint with Giff for a while and as he walks through the main door, he clashes with someone coming out. The two men glare at one another for a moment with hostile looks until Marty swallows hard and nods his head.

"Have a good night Dan." He says, a little nervously.

"Yeah you too." Replies Dan, nodding back at him awkwardly.

Marty hesitantly holds out his hand and waits.

Dan looks down and breathes deeply as he holds out his hand too.

"For the sake of the boy and his mum, yeah?"

"Yeah, for them." Replies Marty, as they shake hands briefly and part company fairly sharpish in different directions. Standing at the urinal, Marty closes his eyes in realization that they will probably never be together. It was never going to happen after the day she got on that train and headed for London. They had been kidding themselves for a while. The excitement of the hotel, the memories of West Way and their teenage love.

If it hadn't been for Alex, they would never have rekindled their love for one another. Dan was her life and had been for many years. He was dad to Alex as well. None of it was his. He remembers the day he was punched so hard by Dan. A day that will sit in his mind always. He wanders over to the sink and throws some water on his face before taking a deep breath and heading back to the gig.

"Hi ya Marty." Says a familiar voice with a tap on the shoulder.

"Hey, good to see ya." He replies, catching sight of Alex by his side and noting that he didn't call him dad this time.

"So glad you came. Mum really wanted you to be here tonight. How are you?" Asks Alex, trying hard to get it right with his birth dad but still feeling a little awkward.

"Yeah I'm ok thanks." Replies Marty. "I'm gonna try much harder to be in touch this year. I'm truly sorry for being a dickhead. We'll meet up soon hey, I'll call you when I can, I promise."

"I look forward to that. Catch you soon." Says Alex, moving off to get back to the where the gig will be and raising his hand to say goodbye.

*****

"Bloody hell, Shell Rogers?" Comes a male voice from behind as she makes her way back from the loos.

Turning quickly to see who is calling her, she looks straight into familiar eyes from her past.

"Oh my god! How did *you* get here? I mean, holy shit, what are you doing here?"

"I knew it was you, Shell. You haven't changed much. Well, maybe a little more beautiful than the scraggy teenager I once knew. Do I get a hug and a kiss then?" He says, with a slight nervous chuckle.

"Fuckin' hell! Tommy Gates! Come here you big old bear you. Too many years since I've seen you boy!! What the hell are you doing here? That's just mad!"

Hugging him tightly, she feels a wave of reminiscence and love for the gorgeous boy she fell head over heels in love with at the tender age of thirteen and the complete madness that they got up to as good friends so many years ago.

"My god, I never thought I would ever see you again. Did you know how much of a mad crush I had on you for years at school?" She chuckles, holding on to his arm. "I could never get any work done and none of the other boys got a look in for a long, long time." She snorts loudly, making herself look like a silly, giggly teenager again with blushing cheeks.

"I probably didn't at the time." He laughs. "But looking back I can see it loud and clear. I knew you left for London. Are you still living here then? Married? Happy?" Tommy asks, with huge interest.

"I'm single now." She replies, a little sadly. "Last couple of years have been a bit mad. Meeting up with old friends. Life has changed so much for me. No time to talk really but would be great to catch up with you sometime though."

"Here, write your address and number on this and I will catch up with you when I can. I'm with some work mates right now."

He passes her a scrap of paper from his pocket and a tiny pencil he'd picked up at the bookies.

"Here ya go." She says, quickly scribbling as she can hear riotous applause for The Specials coming on to the stage. "Be so good to see you again darlin'."

She kisses his cheek and runs off to the stalls to find the others feeling quite loved up again.

The harmonica sound of 'A Message To You, Rudy' has started and battling through the crowd, she finds her mates up on the dance floor already and joins in, linking arms with Lou and Sam lovingly.

"Oh my god this is truly amazing. Skank time with my best old mates. Doesn't get much better than this in life!"

The three girls dance together smiling broadly right through the song and loving the memory.

Shell stares at the stage in awe and at the ageing but absolutely beautiful Terry Hall. She feels a huge wave of love for him and the amazing music the band has given her. Feeling a lump in her throat as she watches him sing and wishing she could hold him for a moment to thank him for the memories, she holds up her hands and waves madly at him like the devoted teenager that she was back in her school days.

As the song ends, the girls cheer at the top of their voices and Shell grabs the girls closely to tell them who is there. "You won't believe this but Tommy Gates is here for fuck's sake!" She shouts excitedly, trying to be heard above the rowdy crowd. "It's mad, I just bumped into him out there. It was as if we had just met up in D block back at school." She laughs, reminiscently.

"Yeah, what's he look like then?" Asks Lou, giggling madly.

"Still fuckin' hot girls. Oh boy, those eyes!"

The three of them laugh together and Sam puts her arm around Shell to speak closely.

"Sorry to tell you this but we knew he would be here. We met up with him a while back in town. He'd been away for ages living all over the place but was keen to meet up with you after all these years. He mentioned he was going to this same gig with some mates of his so we told him to look out for you. Think it looks like he has the hots for ya mate. He's read your book and very keen!"

The whole floor erupts as 'Stereotype' blasts out with heads bobbing up and down, leaping bodies and braces hanging loose on many ageing but ecstatic, sweaty men and women. The girls grab Giff and Tomo to dance and Marty and Daz run in to get amongst it too.

Having the whole gang together feels so special at such an amazing gig for Shell and her throat begins to hurt from singing and shouting at the top of her voice.

The night is completely full of singing and skanking with so many happy memories and love for each other. The Specials deliver a set of all the amazing tunes that made a storyline of their lives.

"We're gettin'old you lot but fuckin' hell I haven't enjoyed a night out like this for ages." Says Daz, still swaying to the last of 'Gangsters' as the gig comes to an end.

"Thanks for making tonight so special you lot." Says Shell, feeling quite smashed. "Love you all forever and we meet once a month now for the rest of our days yeah?"

"Too right we will." Replies Daz.

"Love ya all." Says Giff, wiping the sweat from his forehead and hugging Shell.

"Best mates always!" Adds Lou and Sam together.

Tomo grabs them all into a huge hug together. "Always here for each other any day and any time, hey you lot?"

Giff starts to sing 'Friday Night, Saturday Morning' By The Specials.

It's not often we manage Friday night and Saturday morning anymore you lot hey!" Laughs Daz. "More of a Friday night and home for bed by eleven!"

Leaving the venue, the fresh air feels good for them all as they say their goodbyes and head off to the train station by cab after their amazing night together.

"Terry Hall still hotter than ever then!" Shouts Shell to the rest of them as she heads off. "Beautiful man. Love you Tezza!!"

*****

Untying her favourite cherry red boots and discarding them to the side of the hallway, Shell throws off her scrap jacket and heads sleepily to the sofa. Flopping down and curling up tightly, she smiles at the memory of her amazing night out. Closing her eyes for a moment, she feels so much love for her best friends who have taken her back with open arms after many years apart.

The doorbell rings as she lays there thinking and it makes her jump up quickly. "Who is it?" She asks, through the frosted glass of the front door.

"Gatesy." Comes the voice from outside.

Swallowing hard and quickly patting down her hair and clothing, she nervously opens the door to him. Unable to get her words out, she just beckons him through the hallway and into the lounge.

"Wow!" She says, at last. "I wasn't expecting you to turn up that fast!"

"I've been wanting to catch up with you for ages." He replies, kicking off his trainers and making himself at home. "I read your book and loved it. Not sure how you managed that though. You were hardly ever at school to learn to read let alone write!"

They both giggle at the memory of running out of school to the beach and down the lanes.

"Ah nice one. Do ya fancy a late night beer?" Asks Shell, feeling quite excited to see her old friend.

"Yeah love one." He replies, throwing his jacket down on the hall table.

The two of them wander out into the kitchen and Shell grabs a couple of bottles from the fridge.

"Here ya go. Cheers!" She says, still in shock. "Can't believe I'm standing here in my kitchen with Tommy Gates! Shall we go put some sounds on?"

"Yeah great. Nice little place you got here girl."

"This always reminds me of your house party." She says, putting on the ipod and 'Too Much Pressure' by The Selecter blasting out.

Tommy smiles and the two of them start to dance. Shell starts to sing into the beer bottle as a microphone.

"Still as mad as ever then Shell!!" He laughs.

"Ah ya know I'm gettin' on a bit now so grabbin' the last bit of fun and energy my body will allow."

The track ends and 'The Bitterest Pill' by The Jam comes on.

"I always call our time the cider days." He laughs. "Do you remember the amount of underage cheap cider we did? We drank ourselves into oblivion and mostly threw it all up again!"

"Yeah we certainly did darlin'." Recalls Shell. "We were mad and bad most of the time!"

"I think I missed out all those years ago." He says, softly. "I never knew quite how much you had the hots for me. I was oblivious to it all and just getting hammered mostly!"

"I was crazy about you from the day I first saw you in my new form class at secondary school. I must've been eleven or twelve and by the time I was thirteen, well I was smitten as they say right through until I met Marty. I knew you weren't interested in me that way, we were just top mates!"

Shell laughs at her teenage self and rolls her eyes.

"I still have a little photo of you somewhere. A little black and white one from a photo booth and always thought about you over the years." She sighs. "Funny how things go hey. We are such different people now. Our lives have been on separate paths."

"All the girls were always eager for the boys before they were ready!" She chuckles.

"Shit I'm sorry I didn't respond. I was more interested in gettin' off my face back then. Girls just weren't part of the deal. We were just best mates in my eyes. Us lads didn't have a clue back then." He laughs.

"I'm on special offer now though, just for you if you want me." He takes away her beer bottle and wraps his arms around her waist.

Giggling nervously, Shell looks into his beautiful blue eyes and remembers why she fell for him all those years ago. 'No Woman No Cry' by Bob Marley comes on and dancing slowly, he kisses her softly for what seems like forever.

"So does this mean I can stay the night then?" He asks, with a devilish smile. "Me and you all night together hey, just what it should've been all those years ago."

For a moment Shell feels like she's a teenager in love again in his arms and feels herself melting a little at the thought of being with Gatesy but begins to pull herself together and pushes him away just a little.

"You know it would be easy to say yes let's do that. You have no idea how long I waited for you to kiss me like that but I've learnt so many lessons from meeting up with everyone again and what happened with Marty and Dan."

She pauses for a moment.

"I have so much love for you Tommy but it's all in the past and we are different people now. I also have so much love for Dan and Marty and I think our friendship is too important. We are all oldies now. I want to appreciate those friendships and know that we are all ok and looking out for each other."

She holds him tightly and kisses him hard on the lips.

"We can't change the past and we've got the best memories together." Let's all just have a laugh together and be happy that we have met up again."

"It *was* a fantastic snog though, worth the fifty year wait I reckon! Fancy another?" She laughs loudly like a crazy teenager again.

Tommy takes his chance and grabs her face for a second snog and they both dance together remembering the past.

"Well if we're not goin' down that route then how about this one?" Says Gatesy, pulling out a wrap of paper from his pocket.

"Go on then you bad boy. You know I can never say no to a bit of white stuff." Says Shell, feeling her heart racing already.

Gatesy pours it on to the table and they both giggle together feeling like they did back at his house parties so many years ago.

"And so another crazy night continues." Exclaims Gatesy, chopping the powder finely on the dining table with his old mate and feeling like naughty teenagers once again.

"Oh man, I've missed our mad moments together. We're probably gonna feel like shite tomorrow but I'm up for the laughs boy!" Giggles Shell. "Let's get hammered!"

*****

Slowly opening her eyes and thinking about the fantastic night she had at the gig with her best mates and meeting Gatesy after so many years, she grins to herself and curls up into a ball keeping her memories tight in her mind. Tommy lays next to her sleeping peacefully as she looks at him fondly.

She thinks about Marty and all they have been through together and how her life has changed so much over the last few years. She starts to daydream about her mum and dad and the difficult memories she ran from as a young teenager and wonders if things might have been different if her parents had been around for her back then. She may never have run off to London and life may have been calmer and less scary.

Tommy begins to open his eyes and stretch a little. He smiles at Shell and kisses her softly on her cheek.

"Hangover from hell then boy just like me?" She asks holding her face in her hands and feeling like she's been smacked across the head with a shovel.

"Just a bit but was worth the laughs!" He replies turning over and closing his eyes again.

Shell strokes his hair and heads off to the kitchen to make coffee for the both of them.

Waiting for the kettle to boil, Shell wonders what the others would make of her ending up getting smashed with Gatesy again. It makes her smile to herself and thinks about calling Lou later to tell her all about him turning up.

"Hey boy it's been the best time meeting up with you and all of my old friends, you know but I've gotta say I'm a London girl and the place draws me back every time so all I know is that I will be here forever." She says, passing him a mug with a skankin' rude girl on it.

"Yeah I can see that. It's been so good to see you after all these years though Shell. I'll be there with the others for the next meet up under the clock if I can make it." He replies.

"Cheers!" He says, holding up his coffee mug to her. "Here's to our great night meeting up again after so many years. It's been amazing with the gig and coming here. Nice one! Didn't get me leg over but hey I don't really deserve it after ignoring you all those years ago."

Shell clanks her coffee mug with his and smiles sweetly at him.

"Ha, top night though mate. Don't think I should be still acting like that at my age but I'm still a dickhead at heart." Laughs Shell.

"Anyway, I will always meet up with my friends and really hope I will see you again too but this is my home now and I won't be moving back to that little town that caused me so many tears and heartaches." She says with a sense of closure in her voice.

"I am so happy we are all together again but I think you all know I won't be back. Tomorrow I'm heading down there one last time to visit my Mum and Dad's grave on my own before putting all this to rest."

"Good to see you are doing ok Shell. We'll all be there for ya any time and if you want me to come with you tomorrow then I will, with pleasure."

"Thanks mate but I need to do this myself. This journey has been the hardest but the best thing that could've happened to me and has made me find a way to make peace with that town and leave the tears behind." She says happily. "We will all be best friends for the rest of our lives and our memories will live on in our hearts and through our music. After all, it was the best music ever and no one has friendships like ours, hey!"

"We'll have as many meet ups as we can until we're too old to make it!" Laughs Gatesy. "I'm really happy we've all met up again.

"Time to arrange our next crazy skank up then I reckon mate!" Giggles Shell, and landing him with a rather big and wet kiss. "Just had to do that snog one more time you sexy beast!!"

Chapter 8

The roads seem exceptionally long today as Shell heads towards the seaside town where her long departed parents are laid to rest. She struggles to concentrate on her driving and looks for some music to distract herself from the task ahead.

'Mirror in the Bathroom' By The Beat comes on and she smiles at the memories it gives her of strutting down the high street with Sam and Lou, all dressed perfectly in their scrap jackets and cherry red boots. That Friday night feeling of anticipation on the way to West Way discos and hoping to be served cider at the local off licence on the way.

Those days just a distant memory now but heavily ingrained into her mind. She cranks up the volume, bouncing to the great music in the driving seat. It feels so much easier to get there with this skanking tune full of memories to focus on. Apprehensively, she approaches the area and slowly drives through, trying not to look at her old house as she passes. She turns off the distraction of the music and drives silently along the main road.

Feeling a little stronger in the town than her previous years, Shell pulls in to the local cemetery through the set of huge iron gates and slowly drives up to the special tree that marks the spot where her dear parents are laid to rest.

Not a soul is to be seen through the car window. It feels strange to be alone there with so much death and sadness around her.

Breathing deeply and swallowing hard, she opens the car door, picks up her little bunch of flowers from the passenger seat along with her backpack and takes in the smell of the beautiful red roses she has bought. Walking hesitantly over to the grave side, she ever so slightly wishes that she hadn't come alone. Passing the plots of a few old friends and acquaintances on the way, the ground she walks on feels full of grief and the whole experience fills her with sadness and difficult memories.

The white stone book lays still and open on the small area of grass, looking so very old and weathered with many of the words flaking off now. Shell reads the names of her dear Mum and Dad with the dates alongside of their death and sees her own name mentioned at the bottom for who was left behind. It fills her eyes with tears and she wipes some away with her sleeve as she places the bunch of deep red roses into the little marble vase in front of the headstone. Taking out a bottle of water from her bag, she fills up the pot to feed the flowers and adjusts them to make a pretty display.

"For you Mum." She says, quietly smiling.

So many years have passed and Shell realises that she is now older than her parents were when they passed away so very long ago.

Speaking out loud, she begins to chat as if her parents were listening by her side.

"Well I'm here Mum." She says staring at the open book. "I don't know exactly what you went through before you died Mum and Dad but having your life cut so short in your forties was so sad and unfair. You left a broken family that never coped without you, ya know, and I for one have missed you every single day of my life."

Shell pulls out a crumpled up tissue from her jacket pocket and noisily blows her nose.

"Who knows what might have become of me if things had been different and I'd had you both with me for support, just like all my friends had theirs growing up in this world. I probably wouldn't have run away to London all those years ago like I did."

"Anyway, I've managed ok Mum. It made me fiercely independent and I never relied on anyone, ever. I'm still here with a strong exterior but pretty messed up on the inside. I screw up most things that I do in life *and* in love and I move from place to place, not really knowing where I belong and if you ask any of my friends they will say I've got a screw loose and my life is always chaos!"

She looks around at the peaceful graves in the silence of the surroundings and takes a breath after saying too much too fast.

"There have been times when I've just wanted to stop the world and be underground with you, here. I was desperately unhappy in the house I was left in when you had gone. I want you to know it's been so hard and a lot of it has been pretty shit but today I think I'm getting stronger and I'm going home to London where it feels like I belong. I shall be me for the rest of my days and try to be the best I can to my dearest friends and hope they all forgive me for being an idiot most of my life. Just maybe they will love me like I love all of them."

She sits down on the grass for a moment as if to get closer to them both. The sun beams down on her from above and the heat on her face is a beautiful feeling as she closes her eyes for a minute and takes it all in.

"I have treasured memories of being at home with you Mum. They are few and far between after all these years but you know I will never forget holding on to your apron strings and hugging you so tightly like I would never let you go. I remember being off school really poorly and having your huge cuddles. You would make me your homemade soup and dumplings to make it all better."

She smiles at the cherished memory deeply rooted into her mind.

"Do you remember when we played fish and chip shops?" She asks, lovingly. "We would sit on the black and white tiled kitchen floor together and get out the saucepans from the cupboard. We'd cut out shapes of fish from the old newspapers and then cut long, stick shapes for the chips. We would pretend to cook them in the pans and serve them up to Dad for his dinner."

She chuckles softly to herself and looks up into the clouds above.

"And Dad, do you remember taking me to the old pub next door for a pineapple juice in a glass bottle with a straw? It tasted so amazing to me back then. I would always go off into the beer garden and play with the children who lived above the pub. We'd have a great time on their swings at the back and I would stroke the little rabbits and guinea pigs that they had."

Shell smiles widely. Her heart melting with the memories and wishing hard that there had been so many more.

She takes a deep breath and sighs heavily.

"Well, I love you both from the bottom of my heart and I hope that you are a little bit proud of me. You know I wrote a book and got it to TV. My friends all laugh at how I managed that when I barely went to school but I think it helped me process some of my life story. It started off as a little dream I had to write a book and ended up writing three of them!"

She stands again preparing herself to leave.

"You have a beautiful grandson who would've adored you, ya know. He is the best thing that ever happened to me."

Shell strokes the old stone book and the coldness of it gives her a shiver.

"Please forgive me for running away. I just couldn't cope with the memories here. I'll see you in the clouds one day for a huge cuddle again. Rest easy both of you. You were and still are everything to me. Love you forever."

She blows a small kiss towards the open book, turns with a little smile and walks with pride back past the special tree and gets into her car. She stops and takes a last look around at the beautiful church and greenery. The peace makes her feel calm and settled.

Shell takes a moment to gather her thoughts and puts on some music to help her get moving. 'Sun is Shining' by Bob Marley quietly plays for her and taking a very deep breath and a sigh of relief, she starts the engine and drives on without looking back and heading for home.

*****

Wandering through her favourite places back in London, Shell feels at home again. She strolls contentedly along the Embankment staring at the boats and lovingly thinks of the 2-tone cruise that made all her friends so happy. The river is buzzing as usual and the masses of people getting to and from work makes her smile and feel like she belongs again. Shell looks down at her fish net stockings and her beloved cherry reds and smiles as she takes out her phone and turns on the camera. Taking a selfie by the river, she grins at the phone and shouts "Home sweet home!" as the photo is taken.

"I fuckin' love you London!" She shouts at the river. "You gave me a special place to call home." She exclaims. Someone softly touches her shoulder and she turns quickly to see who it is. Her beautiful boy Alex is standing there with his arms open wide and a big smile on his face. He puts his finger to his lips and quietly whispers "Shhhhh don't say a word." He hugs his mum tightly for what seems to be forever.

"I knew you'd be here. I love you Mum." He says, softly. "You're home now and this is where you'll stay."

"Thank you my darling. I did it, I went to see Mum and Dad on my own. I'm so happy to be home with you. I love you so much and am so very proud of you."

"You know I have some very dear friends and have so much love for a couple of amazing guys but it's time to rest now in my favourite place with my special boy and see everyone when I can."

"I'm very proud of you Mum for going there alone. I know how hard that must have been for you and I'm here for you now." Says Alex, gently. "I think it will make things a bit easier for you to come to terms with."

"Come on my darling boy, selfie time." She says pulling out her phone again and putting one arm around her son. Both hold each other tightly and look up with a smile against the background of the bustling River Thames.

"Say 'I LOVE TERRY HALL.' Says Shell, laughing loudly.

Alex rolls his eyes a little at her ongoing obsession with her musical idol.

"No way. Say 'DOC MARTENS FOREVER'. He replies.

They both giggle together and lift their knees up, holding their boots as high as they can. Shell's cherry reds and Alex's in shiny black.

Keeping the phone up high, they both shout very loudly together.

"DOC MARTENS FOREVER!" And they take a very special photo of themselves.

"Keep skankin' always Mum!" Says Alex, smiling.

"I sadly never got my Terry Hall but I've got something far more precious in life. YOU! My beautiful boy and a lot of amazing lifelong friendships. AND my favourite place in the world, HOME!"

The two of them sit on the wall and look down the river feeling a strong mother and son bond that can never be broken.

"It's been a strange but great journey going back in time and meeting all my fantastic friends from so long ago and recalling all those memories we had back in our day." Says Shell, feeling quite fulfilled now.

"Mum, I have to tell you that there's someone here waiting to see you."

Shell looks around curiously and spots a tall dark shadow in the sunshine propped up by the streetlamp.

"What's going on?" She asks. "Who is here to see me?"

She stands up and slowly walks towards the shaded corner and begins to feel a wave of love go straight through her heart.

He stands tall with a huge smile. Those beautiful eyes and his slick black hair watching her every move. Dressed immaculately in his new jeans with his best checked Ben Sherman and black Doc Martens, finished off with a perfect black Harrington and looking smart as hell.

"Hey gorgeous girl." He says, holding out his arms to her once again and giving a sweet smile and a wink.

"Oh Marty, how did you know I'd be here and what the hell are you doing in London?" She replies, looking quite shocked at the sight before her.

"I'm here because I love you to bits girl and I will go to every length I have to in this world to see you. Even coming to London!" He declares, confidently.

"I want to spend what time we have left in this world loving you as much as I can so if you'll have me, I'll be making this trip every week to see you and my son. We've been through too much together to let our love disappear, don't you think?"

"Oh Marty, I love you so much boy. Come here and kiss me."

"With pleasure." He replies, taking her face in his hands and staring lovingly into her eyes.

It seems to last forever and Alex finally makes a nervous cough to part them.

"That's enough of that you two." He says, feeling awkward next to them both. "Go get a room for heaven's sake!"

The three of them laugh together.

"I have something for you." Says Marty, reaching into his backpack.

He hands her a gift wrapped in black and white checked paper.

Shell smiles at the look of it and slowly unwraps the box.

"Oh my god it's just identical to my old one. It has completely given up playing now!" She exclaims.

"I'll never forget the old days of your cassette recorder darlin'." He smiles. "I had been looking for so long to find one just like it and here it is. Just for you with memories of our special times back then."

"Oh Marty thank you so much I don't know what to say. It's fantastic. I'm blown away and love you so much boy. I can play my treasured Dance Craze cassette on it now!"

"Our music will last forever." Marty replies. "I think we should head for a park tomorrow and sit under a tree with your special tape recorder to blare out the sounds. Take some food and a few beers, hey?"

"I'd love that so much," She beams with affection and kisses him softly on the cheek.

"Come on then both of you, let's go home." Says Shell, happily. "I think I'm ready for the next chapter of my life!"

"Keep skankin' you two." Says Alex, with a smile and a wink for his dad. "It'll keep you both young forever!"

Marty takes her hand gently. "It doesn't matter how old we get, you'll always be my beautiful skankin' girl!"

THE END

Printed in Dunstable, United Kingdom